Praise for *No More Perfect Marriages*

In the years I have known Mark and Jill Savage, I have watched them walk through major challenges with amazing grace—and have seen how God created something beautiful in and through them. Mark and Jill have learned lessons the hard way that we can learn simply by being willing to listen and act. I love how this book combines both of their voices to give us an encouraging and very practical picture of the steps they took, and which any of us can take to build the marriage we're longing for.

SHAUNTI FELDHAHN
Social researcher and bestselling author of *For Women Only* and *For Men Only*

Many people *say* you can fix a broken marriage, but Mark and Jill *show you how*. Through this book, they share their story while also giving you tools and principles to strengthen your imperfect marriage. This is a wonderful resource for every married couple.

JULI SLATTERY
Psychologist and president of Authentic Intimacy

Jill and Mark have come back from despair as they experienced their marriage go over the cliff into a pit of destruction. By challenging themselves to grow and uncover the roots of what made their marriage difficult they give you a model to help your own marriage. Join Mark and Jill on their journey of change as they take ownership, forge new paths, and experience the blessings of perseverance.

MILAN AND KAY YERKOVICH
Authors of *How We Love*

Real. Raw. Relatable. That's what Mark and Jill Savage are in *No More Perfect Marriages*. Whether your marriage needs a makeover or just a tune-up, the Savages' message of hope and healing will resonate and encourage you. Mark and Jill have experienced "for better or for worse," and I for one thank them for being so transparent. They're right—*every marriage is a fixer-upper*—including mine. Even after twenty-seven years of marriage, *No More Perfect Marriages* encouraged me. Biblically sound, culturally relevant, and covenant-minded, *No More Perfect Marriages* is for every married couple!

HEIDI ST. JOHN
Author, speaker, and podcaster at TheBusyMom.com

Not surprisingly, Mark and Jill have written a very vulnerable, honest, and helpful book for couples who sometimes wonder about their "imperfect" marriages. *No More Perfect Marriages* is like having a casual conversation over coffee and sitting through an intense counseling session all in one. If you want to improve, save, restore, or renew your marriage, read this book.

MIKE BAKER
Senior Pastor, Eastview Christian Church, Normal, IL

In the sea of marriage resources, *No More Perfect Marriages* stands out in an exceptional way! Providing honest, straightforward insight, the Savages share how to keep a marriage from entering a slow fade of numbness which morphs into a flat line. With a fresh awareness and authentic sincerity, *No More Perfect Marriages* is a must read for anyone who desires a vibrant, effective marriage!

LAURA PETHERBRIDGE
Speaker, author of *When "I Do" Becomes "I Don't"*, and coauthor of *The Smart Stepmom*

No More Perfect Marriages is filled with practical tools and biblical wisdom that will empower readers to create healthier responses when facing marital challenges. I am excited about adding Jill and Mark Savage's story and wisdom to our recommended resources for couples seeking counseling at our center.

MICHELLE NIETERT
Licensed Professional Counselor Supervisor,
Clinical Director of Community Counseling Associates

For too many years, I thought I was the only one in a "hard" marriage. Everyone else made it look so easy, so perfect, so . . . *happy*. Sure, we had our share of happy moments, but we also had more than a few moments of grueling struggle, hard work, and frustration. With an honest and hard-earned voice, Mark and Jill Savage bravely replace the Hollywood mirage of a storybook romance with a healthy blueprint of a real and rock-solid relationship. If you're looking for authentic story, practical how-to, and hope to build a true and lasting love, you've found it.

MICHELE CUSHATT
Speaker and author of *Undone: A Story of Making Peace With an Unexpected Life*

No More Perfect Marriages is a book that every couple wanting a better marriage must read. With boldness and transparency, Jill and Mark nail the biggest challenges in marriage and offer real, biblically based solutions. I've been married thirty-five years and my husband and I will read it together!

MEG MEEKER
Bestselling author and creator of the online course
The 12 Principles of Raising Great Kids

Couples in all stages of marriage will benefit from this book and its practical suggestions that are based on biblical principles. Specifically, Mark and Jill teach readers how to recognize and deal with seven dangerous "slow fades" that can creep into a marriage at any time. I highly recommend this book and I appreciate Mark and Jill's willingness to share their story in order to help others.

DEB ALEXANDER
Married to Jerry for twenty-six years

Great to see a book written from two points of view, and this makes it a perfect book to read and discuss with your spouse. Sharing your past honestly and openly helps us see and understand ours more clearly. Thanks for the tools for future use! You've kept them simple, explaining their practical applications throughout your book. Your tools are timeless, useful for any stage of marriage.

DON AND CATHY ROBERTS
Married forty-five years (the best is yet to come!)

This book fills a unique niche in the marriage help category. Using the theme of home renovation appeals to the hands on, nuts and bolts crowd, while at the same time offering honest and intimate insight into matters of the heart. An invaluable tool for any married couple. I think Jill and Mark have really nailed it with this one!

ROBYN WILLIAMSON
Married (happily!) twenty-three years

While I would have loved reading *No More Perfect Marriages* twenty years ago, I was happy to learn there are still things that I can do to make my marriage better. Every season of a marriage brings challenges and this book pinpoints those and offers a plan to work through them.

MARCIA FETZER
Advanced Copy Reader

No More Perfect Marriages helped me see and identify the differences between my husband and me. I had to confront and challenge my belief that I was right and my husband was wrong about how we approach life. This book helped me to better understand my husband, and it gave me tools to help deal with these differences. It really changed my outlook on my marriage.

JULIE FRITSCH
Advanced Copy Reader

In their candid, down-to-earth style, Mark and Jill share from personal experience lessons they have learned and insights they have gained from their marriage. This book can help any couple in any stage of marriage build a better relationship. We wish this book had been written before we got married!

SCOTT AND BONNIE MILLER
Married thirty-seven years and still learning about each other

No More Perfect Marriages gave us a real-life, real-time way to discuss the difficulties of being a married couple in today's world. So good to know we are not the only ones who struggle, and that God's grace is real!

NATE KLINGER
Husband, pastor, preacher, worship leader, and pilgrim on the journey

NO
MORE
PERFECT
MAR*R*IAGES

Experience the Freedom of Being **REAL** Together

JILL SAVAGE AND MARK SAVAGE

MOODY PUBLISHERS
CHICAGO

All Scripture quotations, unless otherwise indicated, are taken from the Holy Bible, New International Version®, NIV®. Copyright © 1973, 1978, 1984, 2011 by Biblica, Inc.™ Used by permission of Zondervan. All rights reserved worldwide. www.zondervan.com. The "NIV" and "New International Version" are trademarks registered in the United States Patent and Trademark Office by Biblica, Inc.™

Scripture quotations marked ESV are from The Holy Bible, English Standard Version® (ESV®), copyright © 2001 by Crossway, a publishing ministry of Good News Publishers. Used by permission. All rights reserved.

Scripture quotations marked NASB are taken from the *New American Standard Bible®*, Copyright © 1960, 1962, 1963, 1968, 1971, 1972, 1973, 1975, 1977, 1995 by The Lockman Foundation. Used by permission. (www.Lockman.org)

Scripture quotations marked NLT are taken from the Holy Bible, New Living Translation, copyright © 1996, 2004, 2007 by Tyndale House Foundation. Used by permission of Tyndale House Publishers, Inc., Carol Stream, Illinois 60188. All rights reserved.

Scripture quotations marked THE MESSAGE are from *The Message*, copyright © by Eugene H. Peterson 1993, 1994, 1995. Used by permission of NavPress Publishing Group.

Published by arrangement with Transatlantic Literary Agency, Inc.

Edited by Elizabeth Cody Newenhuyse
Interior design: Smartt Guys design
Authors photo: Erica Gilliam
Cover design: Faceout Studios and Erik M. Peterson
Cover image: Cover photo of wedding rings copyright © 2016 by Jamie Grill/Getty Images (160019044). All rights reserved.

Library of Congress Cataloging-in-Publication Data

Names: Savage, Jill, author. | Savage, Mark, author.
Title: No more perfect marriages : experience the freedom of being real together / Jill Savage and Mark Savage.
Description: Chicago : Moody Publishers, [2017]
Identifiers: LCCN 2016050203 (print) | LCCN 2016051890 (ebook) | ISBN 9780802414939 | ISBN 9780802495099
Subjects: LCSH: Marriage–Religious aspects–Christianity.
Classification: LCC BV835 .S275 2017 (print) | LCC BV835 (ebook) | DDC 248.8/44–dc23
LC record available at https://lccn.loc.gov/2016050203

We hope you enjoy this book from Moody Publishers. Our goal is to provide high-quality, thought-provoking books and products that connect truth to your real needs and challenges. For more information on other books and products written and produced from a biblical perspective, go to www.moodypublishers.com or write to:

Moody Publishers
820 N. La Salle Boulevard
Chicago, IL 60610

13 5 7 9 10 8 6 4 2

Printed in the United States of America

CONTENTS

Foreword 9

Introduction 11

1. Welcome to Our Real Marriage—and Maybe Yours 15

2. What's Your Blueprint? 29

3. Pick Up Your God-Tools! 45

4. Love the Real, Not the Dream 77

5. If It Matters to Me, It Should Matter to You 99

6. When I Said "I Do," I Didn't Mean That! 115

7. The Dishes Go in the Dishwasher Only One Way 137

8. "I'm Not Overreacting!" 163

9. Beware the Quicksand 179

10. Naked But Not Ashamed 203

11. Contentment, Freedom, and Hope 215

   Appendix A: Personal Operating System Inventory 221

   Discussion Guide 233

   Acknowledgments 259

   Connect with Mark and Jill 261

   About the Authors 263

   About Hearts at Home 265

   Notes 267

Foreword

I have been a marriage counselor for over forty years and I have never seen a perfect marriage. I once asked an audience: "Does anyone here know of a perfect husband?" One man raised his hand immediately and shouted out, "My wife's first husband." My observation is that if there are any perfect husbands, they are deceased, and most of them got perfect after they died. The reality is, there are no perfect husbands and no perfect wives, so why would we expect to have a perfect marriage?

It is much more realistic to seek a *growing* marriage. Marriages either grow or they regress. They never stand still. A growing marriage creates a positive emotional climate. We are moving in a good direction. Things are getting better as we seek to understand each other and work together as a team.

However, growth requires nurturing. No plant grows very well without nutrients.

Growth begins by examining the soil in which you were planted. Your family of origin has made a tremendous impact on your mental, emotional, and spiritual development. Husbands and wives typically grew up in different gardens. We bring these learned patterns from childhood into the marriage. These differences lead to conflicts, and conflicts often lead to arguments. Unresolved arguments lead to the building of walls, which makes communication more difficult.

Many couples begin to feel there is no hope; our differences are too great; our hurt is too deep; it has gone on too long. It is at this stage that often one of them makes the decision to escape in hopes of finding someone with whom they are compatible. The tragedy is that the new spouse also grew up in a different garden, and conflicts will also emerge. The divorce rate is higher in second marriages than in first; and in third marriages it is even higher. The answer is not running, but learning.

In this book you will see the real Mark and Jill Savage—not a perfect couple, but a growing couple. You will discover how couples fade into hopelessness, but you will also discover how to turn the "fading" process around into a growing marriage. Decide to have a growing marriage, and this book will give you a roadmap. Remember, climbing the mountain may be slow, but each step up will encourage you to take the next.

GARY D. CHAPMAN, PHD
Author of *The 5 Love Languages*®

Introduction

§ tanding naked in public.

That's what writing this book has felt like for us.

Scary. Honest. Real. Authentic. Freeing. After years of resisting full vulnerability, we're now committed to authenticity both inside and outside of our marriage. We like it better that way.

Getting naked outside the covers has been our mantra since our marriage imploded five years ago. We've dug deep, removed masks, peeled away layers, and found each other and the marriage we always wanted.

Of course, our marriage isn't perfect and neither is yours. We've been married twenty-five wonderful years and we are just getting ready to celebrate our thirty-fourth anniversary. Over the years, we've dealt with baggage from childhood, personality and temperament differences, our tendency to criticize and judge, unrealistic expectations, the ebb and flow of "being in love" feelings, and more. Our promise to you is an honest story and the willingness to share hard-earned wisdom discovered along the way. We're cheering you on to embrace your real, beautiful, broken, less-than-perfect marriage and stay in the game for the long haul.

This isn't a marriage book filled with unproven principles. This is the real stuff of life, lived out in all of its messiness. Here's what you *won't* find on these pages:

Stereotypes. We want to blow those right out of the water. We're not the average "emotional wife" and "logical husband." We're betting you don't fit stereotypes in some way, too. Instead we are committed to help you figure out how God made you and your spouse so you can learn how to dance together without stepping on each other's toes.

Unrealistic expectations. Marriage is HARD WORK. You *are* wonderfully incompatible. You will have conflict. You'll find yourself frustrated with each other. You will deal with things you NEVER thought you'd deal with. This all is NORMAL. The key is learning how to see the frustrations through different eyes and to find successful ways to navigate them!

Perfection. There are no perfect husbands. There are no perfect wives. There are no perfect marriages. Too often we feel we're the ONLY ones dealing with challenges in marriage. You're no different than any other couple out there trying to make oneness happen with two imperfect people. We know you'll feel more "normal" after reading this book.

Pie-in-the-sky ideas. There's nothing on these pages that isn't tried and true. Either we've lived it out ourselves or we've had the privilege of walking alongside another couple who have found a successful strategy and allowed us to share it with you.

We've designed this book to be used in several different ways:

Individually. If you're the reader and your spouse is not, that's okay! Read, learn, and apply—your marriage will be better for it. If your spouse is open to you sharing some of the sections that are particularly meaningful to you, share along the way! There are several quizzes mentioned in the book that help you know yourself better. If your spouse is willing, have him or her take these quizzes too! (You can sign up for our *Get Naked Email Challenge* at NoMorePerfectMarriages.com.)

As a couple. It's a double date with Mark and Jill! When we've read books together, we've done it one of three ways: (1) Take turns reading aloud together each night before turning out the lights, (2) Take turns reading the same book with two different color highlighters (works best with a hard-copy book but can be done with e-books too!), (3) Get two books—read at our own pace and then talk as we read.

As a group study. Appropriate for couples' small groups, men's or women's studies, or moms' groups, the discussion guide in the back of the book will work for all kinds of group settings. To facilitate discussion, there are group videos for you to use at NoMorePerfectMarriages.com!

No matter how you decide to spend time with us, we're glad we get to do this together. If you want to keep the encouragement coming, you can subscribe to our Marriage Monday blog posts at www.JillSavage.org!

Now let's dig in and experience the freedom of being real together!

—Mark and Jill

## CHAPTER 1

Welcome TO OUR REAL MARRIAGE—AND MAYBE Yours

ill remembers: It was our first argument, and it happened somewhere in the Rocky Mountains. We were five days into our honeymoon and had stopped at a campground along a winding mountain road. We set up our tent in the rain and got angry with each other in the process. I marched off up the mountain road, fully expecting him to chase after me. Several minutes later I returned to the tent— not chased, soaking wet, and emotionally deflated. *This isn't what I expected marriage to look like.*

Mark remembers: We'd been married just about two years. It seemed as if our entire weekend was just one disagreement after another. We were simply too different. As we got in the car to head to church, it was evident we were going to be late once again. I absolutely hate being late and I was furious. In my anger, I picked up Jill's purse and threw it on the floor of the car. *This isn't what I expected marriage to look like.*

We're the Savages. We've been married thirty-three years, twenty-five of them happily.

While that seems like an odd way to start a marriage book, it's honest, and probably not so far off from what you've experienced in your imperfect marriage. The blending of two lives into one relationship is hard work. It's complicated. At times overwhelming. It's also humbling, enlightening, and one of the most effective ways for us to grow up.

Most of us entered into marriage with stars in our eyes and a belief that our spouse would meet our needs, fulfill our dreams, and satisfy our expectations. We spent months preparing for our wedding and just a handful of hours—if we had some form of premarital counseling—preparing for our marriage. In our ceremony, we uttered vows that promised we'd love each other "for better or for worse, for richer or for poorer, in sickness and in health," having no understanding of what that might look like in practice.

Reality set in as soon as you discovered this person you committed to puts the toilet paper on the roll backward. Not only that, but they think, process life, deal with conflict, manage money, desire sex, solve problems, handle stress, and make decisions differently than you do. It appears that indeed opposites do attract, and we think, *This isn't what I expected marriage to look like.*

A real marriage isn't perfect. A real marriage is two people being perfected. Come along as we share our story, lessons learned along the way, and discover how God uses marriage to refine us in ways we never could have imagined.

OUR STORY

Jill: Mark and I met on a blind date. We each had a friend who wouldn't leave us alone. "You've got to meet this guy," she said. "You've got to meet this girl," he said. Finally in an effort to shut them up, we both gave in and agreed to one date. I was eighteen; Mark was twenty-two. We were engaged three months later and married ten months later. Yes, we were young and in love, but we married with both of our families' blessing.

Mark: I was working for a glass and plastics family business when we married. I worked a lot of hours, sometimes seven days a week. Jill was a full-time student at Butler University pursuing a degree in music education. We were busy, but happy.

Jill: Eleven months into our marriage, the stick turned blue. We were parents before we celebrated our second anniversary. Two years later, I delivered baby number two on my college graduation day. Needless to say, they mailed me my diploma.

Mark: I had never gone to college and felt called into ministry. So after Jill graduated, we packed up our two-year-old daughter and six-week-old son and moved from our hometown of Indianapolis, Indiana, to Lincoln, Illinois, so I could attend Lincoln Christian College (now known as Lincoln Christian University).

Jill: We lived in Lincoln for eighteen months and eventually moved to Bloomington, Illinois, so Mark could intern at a large church we

. . . .

fell in love with. He finished his bachelor's degree commuting from Bloomington to Lincoln. Eventually we added three more little Savages to the family—two by birth and one by adoption.

Mark: I served as a children's pastor for ten years and eventually planted a church and served as a senior pastor for ten years. Jill started a ministry to moms called Hearts at Home. The ministry grew quickly, and eventually she began to speak and write. We often spoke together on marriage. Our plate was full with five kids and two large ministries.

Jill: Through our twenty years of church ministry, we experienced "for better or for worse." On several occasions we sought out marriage counseling to get to the other side of conflict we couldn't resolve on our own. Mark and I came from very different families. Our differences seemed to be nearly invisible when we were dating, but magnified as soon as we said, "I do!" What differences we did see before marriage we privately thought we could change over time.

Mark: Six years ago, I lost my way. I remember the day I turned a corner in the wrong direction. After a long season of confusion, a hard season of ministry, a change in employment, and my fiftieth birthday, Jill and I were in Florida on a getaway for just the two of us. I was emotionally depleted, disillusioned with God, and discouraged in every part of my life, including my marriage.

We had enjoyed a few low-key days in her parents' condo. On our last day there, all of my emotions collided. God wasn't changing anything in my life that I was praying about, I wasn't where I expected to be in life by the time I was fifty, we continued to have the same challenges in our marriage year after year, and I decided I was done with it all.

I now know that I was living out a full-blown midlife crisis.

....

I came home from that trip resolved to be done with my marriage. Shortly thereafter, a relationship began through Facebook with someone I'd known long ago. Within a matter of months, it had moved from an emotional affair to a physical one. I eventually left Jill to pursue this new relationship. I didn't care what anybody thought. I was doing what I wanted to do.

My thinking was skewed, no doubt. However, during our healing time Jill and I discovered something we call the "slow fade journey." We will be sharing those fades with you, because if I can prevent any husband or wife from dealing with their life frustrations the way I did, my vulnerability will be worth it all.

When I left, I was headed out of my marriage into another relationship. I had a storm raging in my soul that involved Jill, me, the church in general, and my God. I felt completely hopeless that anything in my life could be different, so I decided to take things into my own hands.

Jill: In 2007, Casting Crowns released the song "It's a Slow Fade." The lyrics in the chorus are descriptive of the slow drift that any marriage or any spouse can experience:

> *It's a slow fade when you give yourself away*
> *It's a slow fade when black and white have turned to gray*
> *Thoughts invade, choices are made, a price will be paid*
> *When you give yourself away.*
> *People never crumble in a day*
> *It's a slow fade.* [1]

Mark: We were "working" on our marriage. We knew each other's love languages and spoke them often. We had date nights. We did getaways on a regular basis. We were intentional about communication. In the midst of that much intentionality, infidelity became a part of our story. How in the world did that happen?

THE SLOW FADES

Looking back, it wasn't the big things that made a difference. It was the little things. Things that simmered under the surface. Things unnoticed. Unattended. Untouched.

These unknowns began an unraveling that gained momentum over time. No marriage crumbles in a day. It's a drift of one centimeter to another, one feeling or one decision that leads to another feeling or

No marriage crumbles in a day.

decision that's a little off-center. If left unaddressed, those feelings will draw us away from each other instead of toward each other.

But what if you could see those early symptoms? What if you could identify the slow fade and do something about it before your marriage is in crisis? Or, if your marriage is already in crisis, you could identify the fades you're in and, with God's help, turn things around?

Understanding the slow fades and knowing what to do about them can make all the difference in the world. We've identified seven fades that we have experienced:

+ The Slow Fade of Unrealistic Expectations
+ The Slow Fade of Minimizing
+ The Slow Fade of Not Accepting
+ The Slow Fade of Disagreement
+ The Slow Fade of Defensive Responses

. . . .

❖ The Slow Fade of Naïveté

❖ The Slow Fade of Avoiding Emotion

In talking with other couples — some who just face the daily challenges of marriage and some who have weathered crisis in their relationship as we have — we know that these are common patterns of drifting that every married couple needs to understand, guard against, and correct when identified. Ephesians 4:27 counsels us not to "give the devil a foothold." John 10:10 tells us that the enemy comes to "steal and kill and destroy." When we allow a fade to begin, it is fertile soil for the enemy to begin to divide what God has brought together. If the drift continues unnoticed and unattended, the divided relationship heads in a direction toward slow destruction.

In the coming pages we are going to unpack these drifts one at a time so we can identify any slippery slope you might be precariously near or already sliding down. We're also going to equip you with the tools to turn each one around. Our imperfect marriages are a part of God's plan for growing us up. When you can identify you're standing too close to a dangerous cliff or you've already begun to slide into a damaging fade, that's the first step in getting your head and your heart back on track.

But first, we have to confront the Perfection Infection.

THE PERFECTION INFECTION IN MARRIAGE

Five years ago, I (Jill) wrote *No More Perfect Moms*. This book identified what I called the "Perfection Infection," which leads us to have unrealistic expectations of ourselves and of others, and prompts us to unfairly

. . . .

compare ourselves to others. A year later, *No More Perfect Kids* followed. Coauthored with Dr. Kathy Koch, *No More Perfect Kids* looks at what happens when the Perfection Infection invades our parenting and we have unrealistic expectations of our kids and unfairly compare them to others. From the time *No More Perfect Moms* was released, readers were asking when we were going to write *No More Perfect Marriages*. Now, you're holding the highly requested and much-anticipated book.

So how does the Perfection Infection affect our marriages? To begin with, we live in a world that presents perfection as attainable. We scan magazine headlines in the grocery store checkout aisle that herald perfect bodies, perfect relationships, and perfect houses. We watch movies that solve big issues in two hours or less. We read novels that simplify relationships. We look at other couples in our churches, in our neighborhoods, and in social media, comparing the insides of our marriage to the outsides of their marriages. Too often we arrive at wrong conclusions, feeling like we don't measure up or wondering if the grass really could be greener on the other side of the fence. When our expectations are unrealistic and our marriage doesn't match up to our expectations, we become discouraged, discontent, and disillusioned with our imperfect, yet real, marriage.

Much of what we experience in our real marriage is far from what we see in the stories and images that surround us. Many girls start dreaming about marriage watching Disney movies where Prince Charming falls in love with his Princess and they live happily ever after. As girls become teens, many discover romance novels that paint a picture of what "love" seemingly looks like. Then we find our favorite sitcoms, which more often than not paint love stories of unmarried people rather than

. . . .

married folks. And to top it off we have our favorite "chick flick" movies that unintentionally send messages that don't add up in real life.

For guys, usually we don't spend much of our life thinking about marriage. We do, however, spend time dreaming of the girl. We love to play and experience adventure, and often come into marriage believing that we will have a playmate, a best bud, and a partner for life. Most guys don't think about the expectations of marriage; we just assume it will work out. While we may not be drawn to romance novels, certainly magazine articles, movies, and the media in general color our perception of what a love story *should* look like. If a guy dabbles in pornography (and most guys have been exposed to it at some time or another), his expectations of how a woman should respond, both emotionally and sexually, are greatly skewed.

So if our culture makes perfection seem attainable and sets us up for disappointment in the realities of life, where does the temptation to compare come from?

Start with Adam and Eve. Here were two people in the most perfect setting. They had no worries. All of their needs provided for.

Satan came along and started feeding them lies about themselves and about God. They compared their situation to his lies and decided that their life in the garden wasn't all it was cracked up to be. They acted on impulse and broke the only prohibition that God had given them — not to eat of just one tree in the garden. Despite their perfect existence, they still felt the need for something else, something better. Their children carried on the comparison game when Cain killed Abel out of jealousy. And the saga continues . . . story

It can seem like everyone but us has this marriage thing figured out.

. . . .

after story in the Bible illustrates that people have always played the comparison game.[2]

Unrealistic expectations and unfair comparisons fuel discontent in our real marriage. Most of us aren't even aware of it. We're mired in the muck of everyday life. Defaulting to our unspoken expectations and surrounded by images of perceived perfection, it can seem like everyone but us has this marriage thing figured out.

The Masks That Mar Our Marriages

Then we add in the masks that most of us are experts at wearing. We wear them inside our marriages, fearful of being our real selves. We hold back because we don't want to be judged and we don't want to appear like we don't have it all together. Being a people pleaser is more important than being a truth teller about how we're feeling or what we're thinking. Sometimes when we take the risk to remove the mask, our spouse doesn't handle the honest conversation well. This results in clamming back up and putting the mask back on.

We perpetuate the Perfection Infection by wearing masks outside our marriage. We pretend things are better than they are and refuse to ask for help or seek counseling. Some of us feel that asking for help is a weakness. If we do ask for help, we don't tell anyone because admitting we're in counseling would let others in on the secret that we don't have it all together after all.

Some of our masks we inherited from our family in which we grew up. Some of them stem from our personality and temperament tendencies. Others come from our identity issues. Regardless of where they come from, shame, fear, and insecurity fuel our tendency to wear masks. We tend to hide the parts of ourselves that we consider inadequate or unattractive.

Are some of these masks marring your marriage?

The comedian mask: This mask jokes about nearly everything. Inside marriage, this mask keeps us from taking the things our spouse says seriously. We minimize their concerns and tell them to lighten up. Outside of marriage, this keeps us laughing instead of digging deep at the pain our laughter sometimes covers up.

The caregiver mask: This mask finds its value by accomplishing tasks and being a helper. Inside marriage, this mask is worn by a worker bee who "earns" his or her place in the relationship by doing. Outside of marriage, this mask fuels activity and busyness, often in place of vulnerability and relational depth (if I stay busy, I don't have to go deep in my relationships).

The know-it-all mask: This mask falsely keeps us "in control." Inside marriage, it doesn't allow for differences. Instead of valuing our spouse's differing point of view, we believe our way is the only right way. The know-it-all mask prevents us from being open to change. It allows us to stay stuck and puts the pressure on our spouse to always be the one to change. Outside of marriage, this facade keeps others at arm's length, resisting accountability and deep relationships that can mature us.

The pleaser mask: This mask is worn to keep the peace. Pleasers often lie for the sake of keeping peace in the marriage, but underneath their pleasant demeanor, they often feel resentment. Spouses of pleasers are often shocked when they discover this bitterness. Inside marriage, it is worn to reduce conflict and diminish criticism. Outside of marriage, the

This mask says, "If I work harder, you'll approve of me more."

pleaser mask works to keep everyone happy.

The passive-victim mask: This mask keeps us from speaking up and advocating for ourselves. Inside marriage, it results in an "it doesn't matter" mindset. It also places the burden of responsibility on everyone else except the one wearing the mask. Outside of marriage, the person wearing the "passive victim" mask blames others for circumstances and doesn't take responsibility for their own happiness or holiness.

The overachiever mask: This mask says, "If I work harder, you'll approve of me more." Inside marriage, it keeps us doing, doing, and doing some more, sometimes to the detriment of communication and emotional intimacy in the relationship. It also often harbors a critical spirit. Outside of marriage, it leads to workaholism, overcommitment, and a judgmental spirit.

In our marriage, I (Mark) wore the pleaser mask, the passive-victim mask, and sometimes the comedian mask. I think I wore the pleaser mask knowing that God has wired me to be a servant, but not understanding how to serve and not lose myself. As I unpacked my family of origin, I now see how I wore the same passive-victim mask as my birth father. Which is ironic, because, due to my parents' divorce when I was two, I did not spend much time with him as I was growing up.

The comedian mask always covered up hurt on the inside. It wasn't until I was able to identify the masks and intentionally removed them that Jill and I began to experience a new relational depth.

I (Jill) wore the caregiver mask and the overachiever mask most often. If I am tired or overwhelmed, I can easily default to them even today. Both of these masks keep me from emotionally engaging in my marriage. They are naturally fueled by my Type A–driven, high-capacity temperament and personality type (more on that later!). It wasn't until I was able to identify them and intentionally remove them that Mark and I began to experience the emotional intimacy we both longed for.

Masks provide us a false sense of security. They keep us from truly knowing one another. So it's time for us to get naked. Emotionally naked, that is. (Well, physically naked is a good thing in marriage, too, but that's for another chapter!) Strip down the expectations, shed the pretenses, peel off the comparisons, and offer your whole self to this person you committed to love, honor, and cherish till death do you part.

Throw Away the Masks!

You are imperfect. Your spouse is imperfect. Your marriage is imperfect. Your masks are a thinly veiled attempt to cover up those imperfections, but you don't need them anymore. You can throw the masks away for good. When you kick the Perfection Infection right out of your marriage, there's no need to hide anymore.

So how do we untangle ourselves from impossible standards and crippling comparisons? How do we stop the fades that simmer under the surface? We're going to answer those questions in the coming pages. For now, turn the page, and let's take a look at where it all begins.

⊰ THINK ABOUT IT ⊱

Of the slow fades mentioned on pages 20–21, which one— just by looking at the title—resonates with your experience? What masks are you wearing in your marriage? How do(es) this (these) mask(s) hurt your relationship?

⊰ TALK ABOUT IT ⊱

My biggest takeaway from this chapter was_____

_____

I've never given it much thought, but I think I may wear these masks more often than I realize: _____

_____

After reading this chapter, I'm feeling _____

_____

⊰ TALK TO GOD ABOUT IT ⊱

Lord, digging in to marriage stuff requires me to dig in to my stuff. I confess that's scary for me. I want to pretend it isn't there. I want to look the other way. Yet if I do that, I run the risk of missing out on what You have for me. I stunt my own growth and stop my marriage from being all it can be. Help me to run after more of You and less of me. In Jesus' Name. Amen.

Today's Truth: "Do not be conformed to this world, but be transformed by the renewing of your mind."
ROMANS 12:2 (NASB)

## CHAPTER 2

WHAT'S YOUR *Blueprint?*

*W*e sat in the dark, dank courtroom in a run-down building smack-dab in the middle of Cheboksary, Russia. The judge grilled us with question after question about why we would want a nine-year-old boy when we had four biological children at home. It was obvious he thought we were adopting a child to put him to work.

We patiently answered the questions over and over. It took nearly six hours, but finally the judge granted the adoption and our son Nicolai became a Savage. He was nine and a half and had lived his entire life in an orphanage. We knew his transition would be challenging. Looking back, that was the understatement of the year.

We loved Nicolai—whom we called Kolya—like he'd been ours from day one, but it wasn't enough. The first nine years of his life had left an indelible imprint upon his head and his heart. Our son is now twenty-two and has barely begun to dig in to the abandonment, trauma, and rejection that were planted in his heart during his early years.

Our early life experiences create an invisible blueprint that shapes our thinking, our beliefs, and our behavior. How we were raised, the lessons we were taught, and the home environment we grew up in all formed that blueprint that eventually becomes the framework of how we live our life. Some blueprints, both good and bad, have even been handed down from generation to generation. We carry that blueprint into our adult relationships—including our marriage.

Our framework is also affected by previous dating relationships or, for those who are remarried after divorce or losing a spouse, a previous marriage. Premarital decisions and life experience also contribute to our framework. We all have strong parts of our framework that serve us well. We all have parts of our framework that need some remodeling.

As we look at the Perfection Infection in our marriage—unrealistic expectations leading to unfairly comparing our spouse to others—we have to look at our blueprint and how that contributes to our patterns of relating in marriage. We don't examine our past to credit or blame, but simply to understand. Once we better understand our patterns of thinking, we can keep the parts that "work," and, with God's help, rebuild the parts that need renovation.

Mark's Story

A great deal of healing has happened within my family, on all sides. I want to honor my family and yet provide an honest picture of the blueprint I came into marriage with. As I've already said, my birth father was rarely involved in my or my sister's life growing up. He married another woman and had two sons with her. My mom lived with a man who became my stepfather. For the most part, he was the only "father figure" I knew. As kids, we moved around quite a lot. Sometimes we would live with my grandmother, and sometimes with my mom and stepfather.

The environment with my stepfather was abusive and violent. When I examine my blueprint, the violence I grew up in made me deeply insecure and a people pleaser. That's where the blueprint didn't serve me well, and I've had to do some remodeling. But, like so much in life, there was good mixed in with the bad. My stepfather did teach me to work hard, to fish, to love the mountains, and to be willing to take a risk in the business world.

Before I met Jill, I was living a very reckless life. I worked night and day, partied hard, and pursued one woman after another. I was building a shaky framework for just about every area of my life.

The year before I met Jill, I accepted Jesus Christ as my Lord and began to make significant life changes. I have spent a large part of my adult life working to disassemble much of the dysfunctional framework I brought into marriage and rebuild it using God's truths. I never could seem to get on top of the toxic shame that was a result of the abuse I experienced growing up. After the affair, I was completely and personally destroyed, which was a good thing. I felt like for the first time everything was stripped to the original framework. Then God, as my architect, has been reframing and rebuilding my heart, my relationships, and my life like never before.

Jill's Story

I grew up in a home filled with love. Now married fifty-five years, my parents supported my sisters and me in our varied interests. My sister Jackie loved ballet, my sister Juli was a gymnast, and I loved music. Both sets of grandparents lived nearby, and I was close to both my dad's parents, Mammaw and Pappaw, and my mom's parents, Grandma and Grandpa.

Church was an important part of our family's life. I have fond memories of vacation Bible school, church camp, Easter sunrise and Christmas Eve church services, choir cantatas, and being part of a church family that knew me and loved me.

I seriously thought Mark and I were headed toward divorce the first time we had an argument!

One of the things I noticed after I got married is that I was inept at resolving conflict. I didn't see much conflict in my parents' marriage, so my blueprint told me that "good marriages don't have conflict." I seriously thought Mark and I were headed toward divorce the first time we had an argument!

My blueprint also told me that when the going gets tough, the tough get going. My parents were resilient—I rarely saw anything get them down. Strong negative emotions just weren't present in our home. My tendency to "buck up" and move forward was imprinted in those growing-up years. Because we were told we could do anything and be anything we set our mind to, a strong sense of individuality and independence was formed during that time as well.

While we were raised in the church, it wasn't until I was nineteen and a freshman in college that I moved from religion to a relationship with Jesus Christ. A sorority sister asked me to accompany her on some Amy Grant music. I'd never heard of Amy Grant—but the lyrics of her songs at that time introduced me to a personal relationship with God. This took my foundation of faith to a whole new level. Because I met Mark just two weeks before I started college, we were both growing to know God as we grew to know each other.

HOW DO YOU LOVE?

I (Jill) often remind the moms I speak to that we're not perfect and every one of us will give our kids some reason to sit across from Dr. Phil someday. Indeed, even the most loving home is dysfunctional in some way. This is because families are made up of imperfect people.

When Mark and I were in our healing season after the affair, we learned about something called "love styles." This helped us not only better understand the blueprint we each carried into marriage but also understand the repetitive dance of pain we had been experiencing for years in our marriage.

According to Milan and Kay Yerkovich, authors of *How We Love*,[3] we all bring from our family of origin a tendency toward one or two dysfunctional love styles. We know that doesn't sound very positive, but hang with us here. This was truly a game changer in our marriage! These styles are built around one simple but extremely important question: *Can you recall a time as a child when you were upset and someone comforted you?* Because our early bonding and attaching experiences form our relational framework, our response to that question gives great insight into our relating patterns that play out in relationships.

Mark and I had already done a lot of work on examining our framework, but when we learned about our love styles, the lightbulb went on for both of us. We've seen each of these five harmful love styles in

. . . .

ourselves and in couples we've helped through crisis over the years. We've also experienced the healing that happens in marriage when you move from a harmful love style to a healthier "secure connector" style. Here is a brief summary of each style:

The **avoider** may avoid the messy emotions of conflict. Growing up in a home where emotions were dismissed, the avoider doesn't place a lot of stock in feelings of being comforted. He/she prefers space and autonomy and is highly task-oriented. Avoiders dismiss feelings and emotions in themselves and others and will avoid conflict if they think it will get emotional.

The **pleaser** learned their caretaking role in childhood, and their goal is to be nice and take care of others. Pleasers avoid conflict because they are anxious about rejection and criticism. Dreading emotional distance from their spouse, they will attempt to fix conflict indirectly by doing something nice for you. (Interesting note: both pleasers and avoiders try to avoid conflict. The difference is the avoider can detach and not care, whereas the pleaser pursues to fix everything indirectly.)

The **vacillator** is overly sensitive. As kids, vacillators experienced inconsistent connection, not enough to satisfy. Vacillators are idealistic and look for the consistent connection they missed as kids. They end up angry and disappointed when their high expectations don't materialize. They protest, complain, and easily express anger but are often unaware of more vulnerable feelings underneath the anger.

. . . .

The **controller** fights to maintain control. They often (not always) experienced childhood abuse and are controlling as adults to keep those painful, vulnerable feelings submerged.

The **victim**, also from an abusive home, learned to survive by tolerating the intolerable. The victim takes a passive role to protect against pain, yet is inwardly resentful and angry. The victim is also fearful of conflict.

The **secure connector** has healthy boundaries. Communicating both feelings and needs, they can apologize when wrong, seek comfort when hurting, and ask for help when it's needed. Secure connectors aren't afraid of conflict because they have the skills to discuss and resolve issues, thereby restoring harmony.

I (Mark) am a blend of a vacillator, a pleaser, and a victim. The vacillator in me would draw close to Jill only to not have my expectations met, so I'd then move away from her mentally and emotionally because I was angry and disappointed. The pleaser in me worked to not rock the boat so I wouldn't be rejected. I played the victim role by being "okay" on the outside but resentful and angry on the inside.

I (Jill) am an avoider through and through. The avoider in me shunned emotional intimacy by being task-oriented rather than people-oriented. She also declared that facts are more important than feelings. My strong personality (more about that later) brings in some dynamics of a controller, particularly when I want to make sure I'm keeping my thumb on things that really are out of my control.

As a pleaser, Mark dreaded emotional distance, so he would draw

....

close to me. However, as he drew close, Mark would eventually hit my self-constructed "avoider" emotional fence, which caused him to vacillate—or move away from me in hurt and anger. This back-and-forth movement fed into his victim style as well.

This damaging dance of drawing close and pushing away had us stepping on each other's toes more often than not. We were in a cycle of frustration and hurt we couldn't get ourselves out of and that was contributing to our fades. Once we took the quiz in *How We Love* and began to understand this part of our blueprint, we've both been individually working toward a healthy, secure love style that allows us to dance together without tripping over each other's feet!

I'm learning that there are places in my heart I have never let my husband into.

Remember that defining moment on the beach Mark shared about in the first chapter? At that point my (Jill) avoider "I want my space" love style clashed with his vacillator "I want to be close to you" love style, as it had many times over our then-twenty-nine years of marriage. We didn't know that, because we didn't understand the missteps we were each bringing into the dance of marriage.

I will always need more personal space than Mark does. By dealing with my avoider style, I'm not watering down who I am and how God wired me. Instead I'm learning that there are places in my heart I have never let my husband into, and that was not only affecting the emotional intimacy in our marriage, but also keeping me from being free to be all who God created me to be.

I (Mark) will always be more emotional than Jill. It's the way that God has wired me. However, my emotions were sabotaging my marriage. By understanding my dysfunctional love styles and doing my own internal head and heart work to move to a more secure, healthy love style, I am becoming a better man, a better dad, and a better husband.[4]

If you'd like to discover your love style and learn about how it is contributing to the fades in your marriage, you can find a free online quiz at www.howwelove.com. We recently had our son and his fiancée take the quiz. Their results were fascinating (his love style was more similar to Mark's, and hers was more like me . . . bless their hearts). We were able to share with them what we've learned about ourselves and talk to them about the importance of working toward a secure love style individually to give their marriage a better start. If Mark and I had understood this damaging dance earlier, we might have saved ourselves a lot of grief.

TIME TO REMODEL?

While we were writing this book, we were also remodeling our kitchen. Go ahead—call us crazy. If we can write a book and remodel the kitchen without much conflict, we're proof that God is truly in the marriage remodeling business! We couldn't have done that ten years ago. Those two things would have caused too much conflict! But we digress.

Back to the kitchen remodel.

We live in a 105-year-old farmhouse. When we moved in twenty years ago, we wallpapered the kitchen. Twenty years later, we were overdue for an update, and while we couldn't afford new cabinets or appliances, we were able to paint the cabinets and tear down the wallpaper to give the room a fresh coat of paint. When we tore the wallpaper off, we found seven layers of wallpaper underneath the green gingham paper we had put up twenty years ago!

Removing those layers of wallpaper was a visual representation of what marriage renovation looks like when we peel away our unhealthy layers. We uncover one layer and sometimes find another layer or two beneath that. Some issues are easier to resolve than others. So what does that look like practically? What are some specific steps we can take to renovate? Here are five:

1. Start with you.

Even if your spouse is engaged and wants to learn along with you, resist the urge to identify elements of your spouse's blueprint. Start with your own blueprint. If you're both reading together, you'll likely be able to help each other see things you might not see on your own.

It's possible you might respond to the "Start with you" step with, *Well, that's easy. I'm the only one interested in changing our marriage. They wouldn't even read a sentence of this book.* If that's you, you'll likely long to share what you're learning with a spouse who isn't open to hearing about it. That's disappointing and can contribute to your own slow fade. However, if you're aware of that, you can guard against it. As you read, ask God to help you to see and understand both of your blueprints in new ways. Ask Him to show you how to live out what you're learning and to "share" with your spouse that way.

2. Ask God for help.

When I (Jill) was starting to better comprehend my avoider style, I really wanted to understand where my "buck up" tendency came from. I began to ask God to help me see if there was any place in my life where I learned to avoid emotion. He didn't answer right away, but I just kept praying and asking Him for clarity so I could better understand where I had most likely unintentionally learned to stuff my emotions. Eventually God answered my prayers when He reminded me of two times in my preteen and teen years where I suffered loss and pain that weren't really dealt with. One was when my sister was hurt in a lawn mower accident, and one was when a guy I was dating was shot and killed by someone with road rage. In both of those cases I dealt with the situation by bucking up and moving on. Looking back, I can now see that seeds of my "avoider" love style were planted in those defining moments in my life.

3. Call in a professional.

When we have remodeling work done on our home, most of us call in a professional. However, some people decide to make it a DIY project. I (Mark) have repaired many DIYers' work, or have been called in to work on a home that a previous DIYer had messed up. When that happens it's because someone decided to do something they didn't really know how to do (YouTube videos can take you only so far!). Honestly, it can sometimes be the same when we start with our own head-and-heart remodeling job. We may need a professional's help.

We have worked with both Christian and non-Christian counselors. One of the best ways to find a counselor is to ask for referrals from a pastor or a friend who's sought counseling. If that's not an option, pick up the phone and make an appointment with a counselor you can find in your area. When you look for a counselor, this is what you're

. . . .

looking for: (1) Someone to hear your story, unravel it, and lead you to a healthy, principle-driven direction (preferably biblical principles), (2) someone who expects to work themselves out of a job, (3) someone who will give you resources and assignments to work on outside of your counseling appointment, because the other six days and twenty-three hours matter greatly in the process of marital change. If you meet with someone for a couple of sessions and you aren't comfortable or don't feel like he or she is asking good questions, don't hesitate to go to a different counselor. Counseling draws you out and helps you gain insight into how your experiences have shaped you, good or bad. Good counselors will then assist you in discovering new ways of thinking and behaving in order to have healthy, successful relationships.

When we talk about marriage counseling, most of us think about couples counseling, but there is incredible value in seeking out individual counseling as well. A marriage is made up of two broken people. If we can better understand the "junk in the trunk" we brought into marriage, it can make a huge difference in learning to relate to our loved ones in new, secure, emotionally healthy ways.

4. Tap into community.

I (Mark) first began my head, heart, and soul remodeling work when I was attending Bible college. My neighbor Jim invited me to lunch and conversation. He shared his story, his pursuit of counseling, and invited me to do the same. It was the first time in my life I had ever heard someone talk about counseling in a positive way. I was intrigued by the insights Jim had experienced and the changes it had made in his life and his marriage. I asked for his counselor's number and made an appointment that week.

. . . .

Jim and I continued to meet and talk about our healing journey. It normalized it for me. Not only that, but we learned from each other too. If you don't have someone walking through the healing process with you, you can also look for a local Celebrate Recovery group at www.celebraterecovery.com. Celebrate Recovery is a biblical and balanced church-based program to help people overcome their hurts, habits, and hang-ups.

During our separation, I (Jill) found it important to surround myself with people who supported my hope and belief in the possibility that Mark would return home. I needed a community that believed our marriage could be restored. It's easy for family and friends who want to protect you to encourage you to leave the relationship, but if you hope for restoration, a community that supports you in that hope is very important.

5. Do a new "internship."

Jill and I often call the homes in which we grew up our "home internship." It's where we absorbed lessons in such areas as conflict resolution, money management, communication, God, and a million other things. When we examine our blueprint, we may find places where we need to do a new home internship. I (Mark) had to do that with conflict because the only way I knew how to resolve conflict was to rage and take control. This isn't healthy at all, but I can't just tell myself I'm not going to do that anymore. I have to replace it with something. So I started reading books about anger (and I'm not by nature a reader—I was, however, desperate to learn something different). I listened to podcasts about anger. I talked about it in my counseling. I was determined to not carry this into the next generation, so I did a new "internship" in anger management.

Jill and I decided to do a new internship in money management when we took the Financial Peace University class (www.daveramsey .com) at our church. Taking the class gave us a shared vocabulary, ignited good conversations, and helped us gain wisdom with our money. We worked together to determine how we would apply what we learned to our situation.

Whether it's reading a blog (check out our weekly Marriage Monday posts at www.JillSavage.org), reading a book, taking a class, tuning in to a webinar, listening to a podcast, or attending a conference, being a lifelong learner will help you do a new internship in whatever parts of your life you long to gain more knowledge.

REIMAGINE, REMODEL, AND REJUVENATE

As we've already seen, the Perfection Infection creeps into marriage, revealing itself in unrealistic expectations and unfair comparisons, which in turn cause slow fades that pull husbands and wives apart. Turn to the next chapter to discover eight powerful God-tools that will eradicate the Perfection Infection in your marriage—and help a hurting marriage find healing and a good marriage become great.

✤ THINK ABOUT IT ✤

Examine your blueprint. Ask yourself: *What did my family of origin teach me positively? What did my family of origin teach me negatively?* _____

_____

_____

Of the five steps introduced in this chapter to help renovate your heart, soul, and mind, which one do I need to be more intentional about?_____

If your marriage is struggling: Who could I reach out to for positive support in my marriage?_____

_____

✤ TALK ABOUT IT ✤

My biggest takeaway from this chapter was_____

_____

I took the "How We Love" Quiz at www.howwelove.com and found that I have this (or these) love style(s): _____

_____

After reading this chapter, I'm feeling _____

_____

✤ TALK TO GOD ABOUT IT ✤

Lord, I confess that I was hoping that reading this book would be more about fixing my spouse than about changing me. I know, deep down, though, that I can only change myself.

Help me to honestly look at the blueprint I brought from my home of origin into my marriage. Let me see things I've not been able to see before. Help me to identify places where I should maybe do a new internship. More than anything, give me the courage to dig deep and do the hard work in me that will not only free me from the things that control me but will also change the dynamics in my marriage. In Jesus' Name. Amen.

Today's Truth: "Look carefully then how you walk, not as unwise but as wise." EPHESIANS 5:15 (ESV)

## CHAPTER 3

PICK UP YOUR God-Tools!

I (Jill) was trying to figure out what to make for dinner. It had been a crazy day of taking care of sick kids. At nearly 5 p.m., I stood with the pantry door open, wishing something would jump off the shelf and make itself for dinner. Just as I figured out something to fix, Mark, who was pastoring at the time, called to say he was heading home from the church. "Wonderful," I responded, "would you mind stopping to get some milk at the store for dinner?" He said he'd be happy to.

Thirty minutes later, Mark walked in the door empty-handed. "Mark, where's the milk?" I asked.

"Oh no," he said. "Someone called in crisis as I was walking out the door. I talked to them all the way home and completely forgot to stop at the store. I'm sorry!"

· · · · · · · ·

Exasperated, I lamented, "Mark, you have ruined my perfect plan for cereal for dinner!"

You are an imperfect human being. You are married to an imperfect human being. Two imperfect people who have to figure out money, make parenting decisions, be sexually intimate, take care of a home, make meals, do laundry, deal with car maintenance, and simply live in the same place are destined to find all that imperfect togetherness challenging. When we bump into imperfection—our own and our spouse's—we often don't handle it so well. This is when many of our fades begin. However, we have some valuable tools available to us that most of us aren't using often enough, if at all.

TOOLS! Now you're talking my (Mark's) language! After twenty years, I left church ministry and started Sawhorse Homes Inc., a home repair and remodeling business I had dreamt about for many years. When I'm working on a project, having the right tools makes all the difference in the world. I've found it's the same in marriage. When I use the right tools in my marriage toolbox, conflict is averted, communication improves, disagreements are resolved faster, and our marriage is strengthened.

The concept of God-tools comes from 2 Corinthians 10:3–6 in The Message Bible (emphasis ours),

> The world is unprincipled. It's dog-eat-dog out there! The world doesn't fight fair. But we don't live or fight our battles that way—never have and never will. The tools of our trade aren't for marketing or manipulation, but they are for demolishing that entire massively corrupt culture. *We use our powerful God-tools for smashing warped philosophies, tearing down barriers erected*

against the truth of God, fitting every loose thought and emotion and impulse into the structure of life shaped by Christ. Our tools are ready at hand for clearing the ground of every obstruction and building lives of obedience into maturity.

The Perfection Infection is a warped philosophy that most of us impose upon our marriage. When we have unrealistic expectations of each other and of marriage in general, this sets the stage for disappointment, discouragement, and disillusionment. When we unfairly compare our spouse to others or even to our "imagined spouse," this warped philosophy prepares the soil of our heart for seeds of discontentment to be sown.

Our God-tools help us tear down the barriers we erect in our own hearts. That's honestly where most marriage issues begin and end . . . in the heart. The condition of our heart is directly connected to the condition of our marriage.

Many of the heart struggles I (Mark) have had in marriage were rooted in my struggles with God. Not having a relationship with any earthly father — my biological father was passive and uninvolved in my life and my stepfather was angry and abusive — I've struggled to truly believe God is good and has my best interests at heart. I've wanted to believe that, but the experiences of my formative years made that more difficult.

The more painful our formative years are, the harder it is to grasp our identity in Christ.

How you see yourself is your identity. Our identity is shaped by our early experiences in life. When we accept God as our Savior and Lord, we're introduced to something called our "identity in Christ." We now have the opportunity to see ourselves through God's eyes and we begin to see the world through the lens of faith. The more painful our formative years are, the harder it is to grasp our identity in Christ.

When we try to build a marriage without really understanding our identity in Christ, it's like trying to build a house without the right general contractor. The general contractor not only can read the plans but also has access to the right tools. You and I need God to be the general contractor in our marriage.

The eight powerful God-given tools of courage, grace, love, humility, forgiveness, wisdom, acceptance, and compassion are designed to line our heart up with God's heart. They keep us on track or get us back on track. These right choices strengthen and mature us to become more like Christ each and every day.

TOOL #1: COURAGE

"Have I not commanded you? Be strong and courageous. Do not be frightened, and do not be dismayed, for the LORD your God is with you wherever you go." JOSHUA 1:9 (ESV)

Doing things God's way isn't always the easiest thing to do, but it is always the right thing to do. Courage is not the absence of fear; it is determining something is more important than the fear. Your marriage is more important than your fear of conflict, your fear of taking off your mask, your fear of intimacy, your fear of disagreement, or your fear of honest conversation.

Prior to marriage I (Mark) believed myself to be confident and courageous. I had operated successfully in a family business with responsibilities that included operations, sales, collections, and cultivating new clients. All of these roles took courage and confidence. Marriage, however, seemed to be a different ball game. I found that I was confident and courageous in business but not at home. I'd had role models in business, but no role models at home. Because of this, my insecurity began to surface. The only way I knew how to assert myself at home was with anger; so instead of courage, I used my anger to control. It didn't show up often, but when I felt fear, I responded with control instead of courage. This was after I said yes to God, but before I really understood my value in Christ, so my God-tools weren't gathered into one place where I could access them easily.

I (Jill) grew up in a home where conflict was not engaged. So there was very real fear for me in being honest, vulnerable, and dealing with anything that looked like conflict. Like Mark, I used control in place of courage. However, my control wasn't usually with anger. While Mark's tendency was reactive control, I leaned toward proactive control. I feared conflict and being out of control so I liked my ducks in a row and things done my way. Obviously both of us needed to replace control with courage.

I (Mark) also know that when I don't know what to do, my flesh screams out in fear. Fear most often is fueled by my own faulty thinking and lies that I have believed, such as "I will never get it right," "I'll never be enough," and "I'll never succeed."

Too many of us deal with fear by saying to ourselves, "If I don't know what to do, I'll do nothing." This is a cycle Jill and I experienced in our marriage and we see it in too many others. I don't know what to do so I go passive and do NOTHING. Jill, on the other hand, doesn't know what to do either but she goes active and does SOMETHING. The more passive I become, the more her action increases. I eventually feel overpowered by her strength, which only makes me more passive. Jill wants me to engage, but her pushing and pulling only deflates me further. This feeds my disengagement and is fuel for the fades we'll be exploring on the coming pages. The core of passivity is fear. You're afraid you'll say or do the wrong thing or make someone unhappy, so you do nothing.

Want the good news? You and I have a God-tool to combat fear, and it's called courage. Psalm 31:24 (ESV) reminds us, "Be strong and let your heart take courage." This is one of the hundreds of verses in the Bible that address fear. Having a healthy, honest marriage that pushes through the hard places requires bravery. This is why we have to use our God-tool of courage!

Do you need some practical help to get your courage on? Here are four ways:

Inside Out. Courage grows from God's strength inside of you. He gives us the ability to act rightly, independent of people's acceptance and regardless of fear. I (Mark) have developed my own personal definition of courage that guides me internally: courage for me is "to act rightly independent of people's acceptance and whether fear is present or not."

With Commitment. Courage grows with commitment. We are told in 1 Corinthians 16:13, "Be on your guard; stand firm in the faith; be courageous; be strong." To stand firm requires resolve and commitment. No matter what is happening in our marriage we must tap in to that inside resolve or commitment and stand firm. This is accomplished by knowing (1) marriage is for life, (2) God ordains marriage and gives us the strength to work through any and all issues to experience a successful outcome, and (3) His Holy Spirit will show us how to work through those issues.

Important Note: If you are in an emotionally or physically abusive marriage, you need a different kind of strength and commitment—one that gets you and your children into safety. We highly recommend Leslie Vernick's book The Emotionally Destructive Relationship: Seeing It! Stopping It! Surviving It! *(Harvest House Publishers) and Leslie's website, www.leslievernick.com, to give you wisdom and direction.*

By Choice. We must find the courage and do all that it takes to grow, protect, and strengthen our marriage. We rarely will "feel" like being courageous. We'll have to choose to be courageous instead.

We act courageously in marriage when we embrace reality rather than running from it.

With Action. Courage grows as we act on it. Action added to courage creates change. We have countless examples of courageous men and women of the Bible. Hebrews 11 reads like a summary of courageous people who walked by faith. Each of them faced fear and chose to walk forward in courage. (Can you imagine Noah's fears when God told him to build a boat and there wasn't a cloud in the sky?)

We act courageously in marriage when we persevere rather than quit. When we act with integrity rather than letting our feelings control us. When we take responsibility rather than shrugging it off. When we embrace reality rather than running from it. When we choose to grow rather than staying the same. When we create rather than destroy. When we talk rather than shut down. When we apologize even if we aren't the only one wrong. When we love rather than hate. When we encourage rather than criticize. Get your courage on and push through those fears for the sake of your marriage.

TOOL #2: FORGIVENESS

"Be kind to one another, tenderhearted, forgiving one another, as God in Christ forgave you." EPHESIANS 4:32 (ESV)

Forgiveness is a term we're all familiar with, but it's likely the most underused tool in our toolbox. In fact, if you're married, you probably need to be using your God-tool of forgiveness well over a dozen times a day! This multifaceted tool is how we handle imperfections—our spouse's and our own. It's also how we keep our heart uncluttered and available to God, downshifting our anger so we can have needed conversations without too much emotion getting in the way. Forgiveness is an intentional and voluntary internal process where you experience a change in feelings and attitude regarding a hurt. The result of forgiveness is freedom. You're free from being controlled by the negative emotions surrounding whatever it was that happened and hurt you.

Forgiveness is not excusing. The person being forgiven is still responsible for their action.

Forgiveness is NOT letting someone off the hook. It's letting them off *your* hook, but handing the hook to God.

Forgiveness is NOT condoning. If you forgive, it doesn't say that

. . . .

what happened was okay.

Forgiveness is NOT excusing. The person being forgiven is still responsible for their action.

Forgiveness is NOT forgetting. The action did happen and is a part of the fabric of the relationship.

Forgiveness is a letting go of the wrongs that have been done to you in marriage so you can move on and experience new thoughts, feelings, and interactions. Forgiveness is almost always a crisis of the will. We never feel like forgiving. However, a feeling of relief almost always follows obedience when we do forgive. That's because forgiveness is really about cleaning out the clutter in our soul, our mind, and our heart so they can all be fully available to God. Forgiveness requires us to trust that God is who He says He is and that He has this!

I (Mark) have seriously been stretched in this entire aspect of faith, trust, and love. For me, at times, it has been a crisis point. I have realized that when I am not willing to do what God is asking, I am not trusting God. If I can't have faith and trust in God, then I sure can't love as He does. If you struggle with forgiveness as I sometimes do, dig in and see if it's more of a trust issue than a forgiveness issue.

So how do we learn to use the God-tool of forgiveness more effectively and more often? Here are five ways:

Receive. We can't give something we don't have ourselves. When we accept Christ as our Savior, He forgives us. We keep making mistakes and when we ask for forgiveness, God forgives again. Sometimes we have trouble "forgiving ourselves" when in reality we're really having trouble receiving God's unmerited, undeserved forgiveness. Find

. . . .

freedom in receiving forgiveness and then give freedom in offering forgiveness. Ephesians 4:32 (ESV) confirms that we have to receive before we give: "Be kind to one another, tenderhearted, forgiving one another, as God in Christ forgave you."

Take. Take your thoughts captive. Second Corinthians 10:5 (ESV) establishes this step: "We destroy arguments and every lofty opinion raised against the knowledge of God, and take every thought captive to obey Christ." What that means is we need to exercise control over our own thoughts. We can push our thoughts in the right direction. Too often we sulk, rationalize, and even have pretend arguments in our head. In reality we need to be pushing our thoughts toward love, grace, forgiveness, compassion, and humility. We can't forgive if our thoughts are running wild.

Obey. We have to forgive. God is so very clear in Luke 17:3–4 (NLT) and other verses like this: "So watch yourselves! If another believer sins, rebuke that person; then if there is repentance, forgive. Even if that person wrongs you seven times a day and each time turns again and asks forgiveness, you must forgive."

We have to obey, decide, and then experience the freedom.

Give. Forgiveness is primarily between you and God. If you know you need to address something with your spouse, make the decision to forgive before you approach him or her. This dials down your emotion and helps you have an honest conversation instead of an accusing argument.

....

Ask. When you apologize, don't stop at "I'm sorry." Make sure you finish with "Will you please forgive me?" This brings closure to conflict. It places a question on the table your spouse has to answer at some point in time. It helps heal the wounds you have knowingly or unknowingly caused.

God wants us to know and experience His forgiveness and to extend it to others. Too often we think forgiveness is only needed for the big betrayals of trust. Not so. This is a tool you and I need to use day by day, hour by hour, and on the tough days, minute by minute. (Need more encouragement on forgiveness? Gary Chapman's book *When Sorry Isn't Enough* is a great resource!)

TOOL #3: GRACE

"Mercy triumphs over judgment." JAMES 2:13B

Mark loves his coffee. I love Mark but I'm not particularly fond of his coffee. It seems I find coffee rings and coffee splotches everywhere. In the car. On the floor. On the table beside his chair (he takes the concept of "coffee table" to a whole new level!). After years of dealing with his coffee messes, I've decided to use my powerful God-tool of grace.

Grace is a free gift from God. Because of Jesus, we deserve punishment but we get mercy instead. It's an upside-down response to what we deserve. God gives us grace because of who He is. We don't earn it. We don't even deserve it.

Several years ago, Mark and I became aware of the phrase "grace space" to describe the much-needed tool of grace in marriage. Grace space happens when we allow another person to be human, to make

....

mistakes, to be imperfect, and to have their own idiosyncrasies. When we give grace, it is an internal decision to forgive and a choice to let something go without addressing it.

Grace is a first cousin to forgiveness. In fact it requires forgiveness. However, grace is the tool we need to forgive and really let something go. We use this tool when dealing with the harmless habits that bug us but don't really hurt us. Like coffee. Or leaving lights on. Or leaving the toilet seat up. Or doing things differently than we would.

We also use our God-tool of grace when dealing with our spouse's human limitations. Jill has to pull out the God-tool of grace when dealing with me being hard of hearing and missing things that are said (I often forget to put my hearing aids in after work), having ADHD (I have too much going on in my mind and have difficulty focusing), and having a smaller emotional capacity (I wear out before she does). Do I do these things on purpose? Nope! I do them because I am human.

I have to pull out my God-tool of grace when I say something to Jill and her internal-processing brain is thinking about something else so she doesn't hear me. I have to use grace when she misplaces something. (Jill only buys sunglasses and reading glasses at the dollar store because she loses them all the time!) I use my God-tool of grace when Jill forgets to pack something on a trip. Does she do these things on purpose? Nope! She does them because she's human. Grace needs to be the tool we choose to use to handle our spouse's human nature.

When thinking through whether something needs forgiveness or grace, ask yourself these two questions:

(1) Does this hurt me or just irritate me?

(2) Does this need to be corrected or simply accepted as part of

. . . .

being married to an imperfect person?

Grace is a beautiful gift to give to our spouse, especially if he/she is aware of places where he/she falls short or has bad habits. Grace replaces criticism. Even if he/she isn't aware of the shortcomings, you can use your tool of grace. It's also a beautiful gift to give yourself because it gives you an option for responding to your spouse's imperfections other than criticizing.

When we walk through life as grace givers, we have less stress and are happier. It reflects in our life and actions. I spent so much of the "early years" of our marriage (say, year one through year twenty-nine) trying to change Jill. In the beginning I so loved her strong personality, her decisiveness, her black-and-white thinking, but the same things I loved about her soon began to frustrate me and I started pushing back against those traits. As I look back, I wasn't allowing her to be her. I wanted her to be different. My intense desires were robbing me of life, peace, and happiness. Grace restored all of that to me.

Grace is vital to a growing marriage. Here are three ways to learn to use this tool:

Receive, Then Give. Grace is a gift given to us from Father God, through Jesus Christ. It is His grace we are given to extend to others. "For from his fullness we have all received, grace upon grace" (John 1:16 ESV) proclaims this truth to us. Think of it this way: God will give us His grace to give to our spouse. Wow, what an honorable act. It isn't our grace but His that we give!

Feel the Freedom. When we give grace, we feel the freedom of letting the offense go. This not only affects us but it removes barriers in our

Next time you're tempted to criticize, stop and pull grace out of your marriage toolbox.

relationship. Grace is an internal choice that frees our heart up to love.

Experience the Result. Grace builds up instead of tearing down. Acts 20:32a establishes this: "Now I commit you to God and to the word of his grace, which can build you up." Too often we think lectures, discipline, and accountability do the building. Certainly there's a time for accountability. However, those conversations will be more easily received if there's a balance of grace in the relationship.

Next time you're tempted to criticize, stop and pull grace out of your marriage toolbox. Ask yourself if this is an offense or an irritation. If it's an offense, offer forgiveness before you address it; and if you're simply bumping into your spouse's human limitations, offer grace.

And if you have a coffee drinker who leaves a trail wherever he or she goes, you might want to give the gift of grace, right along with the gift of a sippy cup!

TOOL #4: LOVE

"So now I am giving you a new commandment: Love each other. Just as I have loved you, you should love each other." JOHN 13:34 (NLT)

We get married because we fall in love. Many get divorced because they say they "fall out of love." Because of this we tend to think that love is a feeling. We don't recognize it as a choice, a tool we desperately need to use when navigating our imperfect relationship.

. . . .

Love is a blend of affection, devotion, and loyalty. It is part emotion and part commitment. When you feel like you don't love your spouse anymore . . . that's a normal feeling because feelings increase and decrease in all relationships. When you feel that way, however, it is a red flag that you need to pull out your God-tool of love and start using it intentionally.

When Mark chose to separate and was pursuing divorce, love was my tool of choice. I have to be honest—it wasn't my idea. It was God's. Several days after I discovered the affair and confronted Mark with it, I was despondent and begging God for direction. "What do You want me to do?" I begged. "Lord, You have to tell me what to do. I don't know what to do!" I sobbed.

As I began to calm down, God spoke to my heart. It wasn't an audible voice, but rather a strong sense of direction and peace. "Jill, I want you to love him." Immediately I protested, "But, Lord, he's not very lovable right now." And then God whispered back, "And sometimes you're not either." Well, He had me there. "Okay, Lord," I whispered back, "You're right. You love me when I'm not lovable, so You're going to have to show me how to do that."

A few days later as I was reading my Bible, I opened it randomly to the book of Romans, Romans 12:9–10, 14, 16–21 to be exact:

Love must be sincere. Hate what is evil; cling to what is good. Be devoted to one another in love. Honor one another above yourselves. . . . Bless those who persecute you; bless and do not curse . . . . Live in harmony with one another. Do not be proud. . . . Do not be conceited. Do not repay anyone evil for evil. . . . If it is possible, as far as it depends on you, live at peace with everyone.

. . . .

Do not take revenge, my dear friends, but leave room for God's wrath, for it is written: "It is mine to avenge; I will repay," says the Lord. On the contrary: "If your enemy is hungry, feed him; if he is thirsty, give him something to drink. In doing this, you will heap burning coals on his head." Do not be overcome by evil, but overcome evil with good.

God couldn't have shown me how to love in a practical way any more clearly than that. I began, to the best of my ability, to love every time I interacted with Mark. It wasn't perfect. I particularly remember one night after he left when the toilet overflowed and I called to give him a piece of my mind. Yeah . . . no perfect love here. However, I would say that a majority of my interactions with Mark, God met me in the moment and showed me how to respond with love. Many times I would have to slow down and pray before responding. I needed to *choose* a loving response because I usually wasn't feelin' it in those moments.

During my (Mark's) affair and while I was separated from Jill and the kids, I would meet on occasion with Jill for dinner. It was my request, and my sole reason for it was to recognize we had five children and three grandchildren together and we needed to be able to separate and divorce amicably for their sake. Jill later told me that most of the people around her counseled her not to meet me. She said, however, that when she prayed, God said *go*. I'm so glad she listened to Him.

Every interaction we had she was so unbelievably kind to me. I noticed and was a bit thrown off. I certainly didn't deserve it. Don't get me wrong, Jill was still strong in her boundaries, but she was completely loving and kind. One evening, about eight weeks after I left, I asked her how she could treat me so kindly after all I had done. She looked at me, paused for a moment, and said, "I don't know, Mark, it's unhumanable."

We both started to laugh because she'd obviously made up that word. She later said that she had never thought of that word but it had just come out of her mouth when she had paused and prayed before responding to my question. I asked what "unhumanable" meant, and she said, "It's not me. It's God."

I (Jill) went home that night, pulled out my Bible, and wrote the word "Unhumanable" in the margin next to Romans 12:9–21. It was a perfect word to describe how the Holy Spirit was leading me and showing me how to love deeper than ever before. I learned it's easy to love someone who is loving you. It's a completely different ball game to love someone who is not loving you back.

My friend Juli says that what I did was "invite with love." Mark would agree. He felt that. After he returned home, I shared Romans 12 with him. After he read it, he said, "That's what you did! You heaped burning coals on my head! What I mean is that you treated me better than I deserved and your Holy Spirit unhumanable love moved my heart."

Never underestimate the power of your God-tool of love.

TOOL #5: HUMILITY

"Do nothing from selfish ambition or vain conceit. Rather, in humility value others above yourselves." PHILIPPIANS 2:3

Our human nature wants to do what *we* want to do. Pride so easily sneaks in and does a number on our marriage. It's self-centered. Self-focused. Self-preserving. It's all about "I" and "me." Pride keeps us from apologizing when we're wrong. It builds walls, crushes kindness, and kills intimacy.

Pride is a thief. It robs us of our joy because we are obsessed with believing we deserve something better than what we have. It cheats us of God's plan for our life because we demand our own way. Pride robs us of knowledge because we already know it all. It keeps us from experiencing healing because we refuse to forgive, and we wouldn't dream of admitting we are wrong. It steals intimacy from our relationship with God because "I can do it myself." It damages relationships with others because "I'm right and you're wrong." It keeps us from experiencing emotional depth in our marriage because we are unwilling to be honest and transparent. More than anything, pride wraps a tight chain around our heart, keeping us bound up with anger, demands, and a spirit of unforgiveness. It poisons and robs us of the joys of life.

Although humility feels weak, the truth is that humility is a sign of great strength. It's about putting ego aside. The word *humility* comes from the Latin word *humilitas*, which means grounded or low. When we are "grounded," we aren't easily swayed. We stand firm in who we are, who we belong to, and who we are committed to be going forward. A grounded person isn't looking for recognition, because they are at peace with their worth in God's eyes.

Humility is also about submission. A humble person submits to authority. Submission is not a word that many of us embrace, but when we allow God to lead our life, we submit to His leadership. We do this because we trust Him as our Creator and we believe He has our best interests in mind. The more we are able to submit, the more peace we experience.

I (Mark) struggle with the "submitting" side of humility. Questioning

. . . .

if God really does have my best interests at heart, I wrongly try to take the lead in my life. I have to pull out my God-tool of humility when I'm trying to take matters into my own hands and making a mess of it all.

I (Jill) have to pull out my God-tool of humility most often when Mark and I are disagreeing or I'm frustrated with him. Pride can so easily slip in when I think my ways are the best ways. Pride also shows up when I'm wrong and I need to own my stuff and apologize. My stubborn pride keeps my heart separated from Mark's heart when I'm unwilling to pull *Our flesh wants to argue, protect, and be right.* out my God-tool of humility and use it as it's meant to be used. When I replace pride with humility, it turns around so many marriage fades!

So how do we grow in humility? Here are three steps:

Choose. Just like forgiveness, we rarely "feel" like being humble. Our flesh wants to argue, protect, and be right. We have to actively choose to replace our pride with humility. We have to choose to submit to God and His ways.

James 4:10 gives us this direction: "Humble yourselves before the Lord, and he will lift you up." At the end of my affair, I (Mark) came to a place where I chose to be completely humbled by my sin, my hurt, my thoughts, and decisions. I came to the place where no one could fix any of this but God the Father, and I submitted more fully than I ever had before. I knew I needed to follow and do whatever He led me to do. I've also seen the second part of the James 4:17 verse (being lifted up) come to fruition. My marriage is restored, my family is together, I've regained my kids' trust, and I'm serving God as obediently as I know how. In God's economy, I'd call that "lifted up."

. . . .

Watch. Watch your thoughts. Romans 12:3 reminds us, "Do not think of yourself more highly than you ought, but rather think of yourself with sober judgment, in accordance with the faith God has distributed to each of you." When we are humble we stop thinking of our plan, our hurt, our decisions, our will, our wants, our desires; and we completely move to the place of thinking of what God wants and His will. When we're frustrated with our spouse, it's helpful to ask, "So have I ever done anything like this?" Often the answer is yes and when you remind yourself you're not perfect either, it helps you get to humility.

Nobody comes into marriage knowing how to be married.

See. When you use the God-tool of humility, look for the impact it makes. Oftentimes our humility softens our spouse's heart in some way. Sometimes it helps to resolve conflict. Almost always it changes our heart and how we look at something.

TOOL #6: WISDOM

"If any of you lacks wisdom, you should ask God, who gives generously to all without finding fault, and it will be given to you." JAMES 1:5

Nobody comes into marriage knowing how to be married. We might *think* we know, but it doesn't take long to realize "you don't know what you don't know." Even if you had good role models growing up, there's much you didn't see that contributed to a lifelong marriage. The wrong little choices pull us apart and the right little choices keep us connected. It's our God-tool of wisdom that keeps us making the right little choices.

....

Learning about marriage is a lifelong journey. Even couples that have been married for decades need to keep seeking wisdom on how to be the right person, how to better understand the differences, how to deepen intimacy both sexual and nonsexual, how to stop the fades, and how to handle anything that life throws our way.

We gain wisdom from the Bible, from the knowledge and experience of wise people, and from our own experiences. Some people look at the Bible as a book of rules. What we need to see, however, is a book where we can find direction and guidelines that can help protect us from the consequences of foolish choices. Living life God's way doesn't protect us from bad things happening in our life; this is a broken world, after all. But we can do our part to equip ourselves. Through God's Word. We also learn from the knowledge and experience of other people. Mark and I hope that by sharing our journey and the lessons learned from our experience, you can gain knowledge that will strengthen your own marriage. And, of course, you can . . . and should . . . learn from your own experiences, good and bad. As you begin to change the way you respond in your marriage, your knowledge will increase!

Right now, we both feel it's important to stop and talk to those of you who are married and your spouse wants nothing to do with making your marriage any different than it is. Maybe you feel like, "What's the use? I'm the only one truly making an effort here. Why am I trying so hard when they don't seem to be?" Before we go any further, there's an important piece of God's wisdom you need to focus on. It's found in Colossians 3:23 (NLT): "Work willingly at whatever you do, as though you were working for the Lord rather than for people." No matter what your spouse does, you have to be motivated by doing the right things for God. Not for a specific result, but simply because God asks you to do things His way. The beautiful thing about this is that you will gain wisdom. You will be changed. And if one person changes in a marriage, the marriage changes!

Even when I (Jill) was learning to love deeper and trust God more when Mark was gone, I wasn't sure he would ever return. In fact, those around me were encouraging me to face the reality that Mark's heart seemed to be getting harder, not softer. I considered whether this was a waste of my time and effort until God reminded me that I needed to be doing this for Him and no one else. I had an audience of One who mattered most. I finally got to a point where I said, "God, whether my marriage makes it or not, I know this isn't wasted. I want to be able to say I walked with integrity. I want to be able to say that I've learned more about You, Your Word, and myself along the journey." If you're in that same spot, step onto the stage of your marriage for your audience of One. The wisdom you will discover will not be wasted.

Much of the mess I (Mark) made in our marriage happened because I disregarded the wisdom from God's Word. I knew what God said about anger being out of control (Ephesians 4:26) but I still let anger consume me. I knew that God's Word said that if I looked at a woman lustfully God considers that committing adultery in my heart (Matthew 5:28), but I still clicked on pornography. I knew it wasn't wise to talk to an old female friend on Facebook (1 Corinthians 16:13), but I did anyway, and those conversations fanned the flames of an affair. In other words, wisdom was a tool in my marriage tool belt I knowingly chose not to use. Sure, I wasn't thinking of that in the moment . . . or maybe I was, but I was choosing to ignore that still small voice of wisdom and accountability in my head.

Humility and wisdom go hand in hand. In fact, Proverbs 13:10 tells

. . . .

us, "Where there is strife, there is pride, but wisdom is found in those who take advice." Humility allows us to hear the wisdom of others. Humility opens our heart to the wisdom of God's truth. Humility lets us take a hard look at our experiences and determine whether we should repeat the same actions or run in the opposite direction!

Here are three practical ways to grow in wisdom:

Look to the Word. If you've never read much of the Bible, a great book to start with is the book of Proverbs, known as the Book of Wisdom. A great habit to get into is to start reading the chapter in Proverbs that corresponds to the day of the month. If today is the fifth of the month, read Proverbs 5, then tomorrow Proverbs 6. If you miss a day, don't worry. Just pick up on whatever Proverbs chapter matches the day of the month. There are thirty-one chapters in Proverbs, so when you get to the end of the month, start Proverbs over again. You can never get too much wisdom!

Listen to the Spirit. The Holy Spirit leads and guides. Much of the time we're just not listening. Pay attention to the moments when you get a true feeling of guilt. Maybe you spoke harshly to your spouse and you knew that wasn't necessary and now you need to apologize. Trust those times when God taps you on the shoulder in accountability and whispers, "Your tone was disrespectful there and you know it."

Lean into community. Letting others in on your struggles can offer both wisdom and accountability. Just knowing you're not alone can make a huge difference in how you feel about the challenge you're

. . . .

facing. Look for others who are honest about their struggles and willing to share lessons along the way on blogs, in books, and at Christian seminars. This is why Mark and I do our Marriage Monday blog posts. You can subscribe at www.JillSavage.org!

TOOL #7: COMPASSION

"Put on then, as God's chosen ones, holy and beloved, compassionate hearts, kindness, humility, meekness, and patience, bearing with one another and . . . forgiving each other." COLOSSIANS 3:12–13 (ESV)

I (Jill) have already talked about how I tend to be a "buck up" person. That means I'm a buck-up mom and a buck-up wife—which means I've been pretty low on compassion. That also means this is one place God has been growing me in a huge way. For years I claimed that, "This is just the way God made me." Then I did a study on the character of God. When I got to "God is compassionate," I gulped with conviction. If God is compassionate and I'm created in the image of God, then that means I can become compassionate. Over time I've come to understand compassion really is one of our much-needed God-tools for marriage!

Author and speaker Tammy Maltby shared with me, "Compassion is a choice. We must choose to see. We must choose to reach out to the other person and weep when they weep. We use our tears and pain to relate, to build a bridge into another person's reality. It is one of God's most powerful tools."

Compassion feels. It builds bridges. Compassion creates a sense of safety and security in your marriage and in the relationships that mean the most to you. Learning to listen with empathy helps your spouse trust you more. It causes him/her to feel validated and loved. Compassion helps you slow down, tune in, and really connect to those you love. It's a God-tool that's so underused in marriage, particularly as stress increases, margin decreases, and you become more familiar with your spouse's imperfections. Closely related to compassion is kindness and patience. In fact, it's safe to say that if you're using your God-tool of compassion, you'll be more likely to be kind and patient, as well.

When Mark went through his midlife crisis, God used those nine months to grow me in compassion. Initially I was hurt and angry, of course. Soon, however, I began to see Mark as confused and hurting. He wasn't the enemy but instead was being blinded by the enemy. He had lost his way. I believe the more I used the God-tool of compassion, the more it opened me up to love "unhumanably." Need to increase your use of the God-tool of compassion? Here are three practical ways:

Focus on the feelings, not a solution. This is where the old adage, "People don't care how much you know until they know how much you care," comes into play. You don't have to agree with emotions when you validate them. You simply have to let the other person know you are connecting to the reality of what they're feeling.

> *You don't have to agree with emotions when you validate them.*

Look at your spouse through God's eyes. See them as broken. Wounded. In process. In need of a Savior. Struggling. Lost. Confused. Imperfect. See them through eyes of grace and love.

Respond with empathetic, validating statements. "I bet that was so disappointing," or "I'm sure that hurt your heart deeply," or "That breaks my heart. I would imagine it broke yours," or "I'm so sorry. I'm sure that was painful for you to experience." These kinds of caring responses let your spouse know they are heard and cared for.

Several years ago, I (Jill) was teaching my No More Perfect Kids workshop at a church. I talked about compassion in parenting and how important it is to relate with compassion with your kids. At the end of the session, I had a mom come talk to me in tears. "When you were talking about compassion," she said, "God took my focus to my marriage. My husband lost his job six months ago when the company he was with restructured. Every day I ask him what he's done to find a job. How many résumés did you send out? Who did you email? Never once have I thought about how he might be feeling in this hard season. I've never tried to feel—I've only barked orders to fix. I'm going home today to apologize and build a bridge from my heart to his with compassion. Thank you for helping me to see this."

That, my friend, is what the God-tool of compassion looks like in real married life.

TOOL #8: ACCEPTANCE

"Accept one another, then, just as Christ accepted you, in order to bring praise to God." ROMANS 15:7

Every human being has a core need to belong. We want to know that people believe in us, approve of us, and accept us for who we are. Acceptance seems to be pretty easy when we're dating. After marriage, acceptance gets harder because we bump into those differences more often! On top of that, we begin to deal with life circumstances we weren't necessarily expecting. This is why we need our God-tool of acceptance.

Acceptance is the action of fully receiving someone for who they completely are without trying to change, alter, or correct them. This is a hard one for many of us. We say we accept our spouse, but in those dark places of reality, we're trying to change them. They are driving us nuts and we want it to stop. This was honestly at the core of my (Mark's) disillusionment with my marriage when I left. I couldn't see it then, but I see it clearly now.

Both Jill and I have had quite a learning curve when it comes to the tool of acceptance. Here are each of our stories:

We say we accept our spouse, but in those dark places of reality, we're trying to change them.

Jill's Story

Acceptance is a God-tool I've had a hard time remembering to use. My pride of thinking my way is the right one too often gets in the way. I want Mark's brain to work like mine, and when it doesn't, my tendency is to criticize or to try to change him. I want Mark to like some of the same things I like and when he doesn't, I work to change his perspective. When I'm doing those kinds of things, I'm not accepting him for who he is and how God made him.

Here's what I've learned: Mark's imperfections are my teachers. They teach me about love and grace and forgiveness and all the other ways God has given me to deal with this imperfect world around me. I do want to be Mark's cheerleader, but I have to not only see the potential but also celebrate the present. I need to see the steps he's taken instead of only seeing the steps he's yet to do. I need to celebrate how far he's come and really see him for who he is, not who I want him to be.

Acceptance has helped me honor my husband. It's helped me celebrate who he is. Mark moves at a different pace than I do, so I'm learning to honor his slower steps forward, even his pauses to stop and smell the flowers along the way. I'm not his mom. I'm not his coach. I'm not his teacher. I'm his wife, and acceptance has helped me to link arms with the man I love in order to walk through life together.

Mark's Story

As I worked through the affair and examined the "whys" behind what happened in my head and my heart, I realized I wasn't accepting Jill for who she is. Instead, I was working against her, trying to change her into what was easier and more comfortable for me. I was working to make her into who I wanted her to be.

My first step in learning to use the tool of acceptance was asking God for forgiveness. I cleaned up the mess I made in my head and my heart against my wife. Once I cleaned up my inside mess, I then asked Jill for forgiveness. Then the real work began for me. I had to start seeing the good in Jill . . . even in the things that frustrated me.

There is so much good in our differences, but before I learned about acceptance, I couldn't see those things. Not only that but I took our challenges personally. I made things about me that, while they affected me, weren't about me at all.

Here's a chart that shows how I changed perspective:

. . . .

THE TRAIT I DON'T LIKE:	WHY I DON'T LIKE IT:	WHAT IS GOOD ABOUT IT OR WHAT I CAN DO ABOUT IT:
Strong personality	Her strength gives me the feeling of not being needed, and it feeds into my toxic shame of not being enough.	I have to stop taking her strength personally, deal with my toxic shame, and embrace my own, but different, strengths.
High capacity	I can't keep up with her. Even though I don't want to, I have to stop long before she does.	I have to communicate, accept my limits, and be fully okay with them. I also have to recognize my medium-low capacity brings a balance to Jill's life, too.
Decisive communication	I often feel parented and inadequate.	Jill is a good thinker. She puts her thoughts in order. She makes good decisions. I can learn to work with her and come to better decisions.
Black-and-white thinking	I am more of a gray thinker, look at the many options, and then decide.	Sometime more options isn't a good thing. A decision needs to be made based upon the facts at hand. Adding more facts can create confusion. Jill balances me in that.
Leadership style	Jill has more of an authoritative style where I tend to be more consensus-seeking. I don't like to be told what to do.	I have to look at why I take this personally and work to be cooperative and not combative.
Direct	Jill is direct in her communication and I don't like confrontation or conflict.	I have to fully accept that direct communication is clear and okay. I have to stop reading conflict into it. If her style crosses the line from direct to disrespectful, I need to communicate that.

. . . .

I confess I am the guy who is always wanting the "easy button." I have always desired the "no combat and no conflict zone." But I'm also the guy who just went along for the ride, not wanting to make waves, but simmering beneath the surface. In the hundreds of conversations I've had with men in crisis, I know I'm not alone.

I remember a time many years ago when Jill and I were not in agreement. The specifics aren't important, but I remember that I finally clearly spoke my disagreeing thoughts to her and she hauled off and kissed me! Yes, you read that correctly. She kissed me! She then said, "I have been waiting our whole married life for you to give me an opinion and find your voice. Thank you!" Obviously it took me a few more years to really find my voice, but I have. Some of you are like me, and you've (wrongly) decided that passive is just easier. But easier isn't always better. Begin to accept and see your wife through different eyes so you can link arms and walk through life together.

✦ THINK ABOUT IT ✦

Do I have a strong enough tool belt (my identity in Christ) in place? If not, what steps do I need to take to strengthen that? _____

_____

_____

Of the eight tools listed in this chapter, which one do I need to start focusing on first? _____

_____

What is the first practical step I can take to help make that happen? _____

_____

Make a three-column chart

Identify your spouse's personality traits that you need to accept and reframe:

THE TRAIT I DON'T LIKE IN MY SPOUSE:	WHY I DON'T LIKE IT:	WHAT IS GOOD ABOUT IT OR WHAT I CAN DO ABOUT IT:

⟐ TALK ABOUT IT ⟐

My biggest takeaway from this chapter was _____

_____

After reading this chapter, I think I need to focus on the tools of _____ and _____

What do you think? _____

_____

✣ **TALK TO GOD ABOUT IT** ✣

Lord, I've never thought about these eight tools You've given me to deal with the imperfections in my marriage. Help me to change the way I respond to _____'s imperfections. Bring to mind the tool I need to use in my moments of frustration. I want to respond the way You want me to respond instead of reacting in the way I feel like reacting. In Jesus' Name. Amen.

Today's Truth: "We use our powerful God-tools for smashing warped philosophies, tearing down barriers erected against the truth of God, fitting every loose thought and emotion and impulse into the structure of life shaped by Christ."
2 CORINTHIANS 10:4–5 (THE MESSAGE)

## CHAPTER 4

LOVE THE *Real,* NOT THE *Dream:*

THE SLOW FADE OF UNREALISTIC EXPECTATIONS

We were married June 25, and Mark's birthday was one month later on July 25. I made plans to celebrate his birthday the only way I knew: with a homemade cake and having family over for dinner. There was one problem with this plan: the way I knew wasn't the way Mark's family celebrated birthdays. They always had a store-bought cake (with those little candy letters spelling out "Happy Birthday") and they went out to dinner. Mark expected his birthday to be celebrated the way he was accustomed to. The only problem with that was that I didn't know what he was anticipating. Oh, the joy of expectations!

. . . .

Most of us have no idea of the hopes that lurk in the back of our minds. Many expectations are unknown and therefore unspoken. That means they're unmet and often unrealistic. Here's our story:

Mark: I didn't realize coming into marriage how much idealism and unrealistic expectation drove my everyday thinking and perspective.

I've always struggled wanting our relationship, our perspectives, and our interests to be different than what they were. We noticed very little of our differences while dating, but a few were evident. After we got married, those differences were suddenly magnified. Even in the early years I struggled with our differences. After nearly thirty years of marriage, I was growing weary of those challenges and felt I didn't have the energy or desire to manage them anymore.

Most of us have no idea of the hopes that lurk in the back of our minds.

Jill: I knew marriage was hard work, I knew navigating differences was part of the territory, so I didn't struggle with unrealistic expectations as much as Mark did. However, I completely underestimated how much Mark's idealism was causing a slow fade in his heart. When he would express his frustration about our differences, I dismissed his concerns and didn't give them the time and energy they deserved. I often reminded him that was normal for any couple. Knowing that was enough for me to remain motivated to stay in the game, but it wasn't for Mark.

Mark: I'm a feeler. I process life through my emotions. I'm an external processor, which means I need to talk things out. I'm also a "medium-capacity" person—I wear out faster than Jill. And then there's the idealist in me. I dream . . . a lot.

. . . .

Jill: I'm a thinker. I process life logically. I'm an internal processor, which means I think about things . . . a lot. I'm a high-capacity, fiercely loyal person. I stay in the game no matter what. And I'm a realist. I'm quick to figure out the illogical side of dreams.

Mark: When my expectations weren't met, my fade led into disappointment and discouragement. For years I harbored these feelings, which, unaddressed, moved into disillusionment and finally detachment, which is what allowed me to eventually leave my family. I didn't realize how much I was detaching in my mind. It happened one centimeter at a time. I was nursing the disappointment, feeding the disillusioning thoughts, and rationalizing why I deserved something different in order to be happy. In doing so, I pulled away from Jill and my commitment to my marriage without even realizing it.

That's a pattern Jill and I see in many marriages: the man who could do no wrong before kids can do no right after kids.

It wasn't until my unrealistic expectations began to impact my "affair relationship" just as they had my marriage that I had to come face-to-face with my idealism. My expectations really were off the charts.

Jill: My unrealistic expectations were more about my husband in general. I expected him to think more like me. I expected him to see things logically, as I did. If I'm fully honest, I thought my way was the right way and his way was the wrong way (can you say "pride"?). So I expected him at some point to see the error of his ways.

Mark: I felt that judgment from Jill. Too often it felt like I couldn't do anything right. I really didn't feel that until the kids came along. In fact, that's a pattern Jill and I see in many marriages: the man who could do no wrong before kids can do no right after kids.

. . . .

Jill: Expectations fall into several categories including unknown, unspoken, unrealistic, and unmet. The more we recognize our expectations, the better we can address them. Let's unpack this dangerous fade and what we can do about it.

UNKNOWN EXPECTATIONS

We recently overheard two empty-nest moms talking about the difference between going to their daughter's house and their daughter-in-law's house. One mom said that when she went to her daughter's house, she could usually find things because they will be stored in a similar way to her own home. Like mother, like daughter. The other mom agreed and said, "But when I go to my son's home, it's different. Things are stored the way my daughter-in-law's mother did things and I can't find anything!"

"Unknown expectations," as we call them, often come from our family of origin. These are the traditions, routines, and habits that are "normal" to each of us. When you spend twenty or so years doing things a certain way, you don't give much thought that there might be other ways to fold sheets, store kitchen appliances, put the toilet paper on the roll, celebrate birthdays and holidays, handle conflict, prepare food, and more.

Because these are everyday routines that are "normal" to you, you expect your spouse to do things the same way. Very few of us give any thought to other ways of doing things, and that's why these kinds of expectations are unknown. We don't even know they exist in the recesses of our mind — until our spouse does them differently and bumps into our expectations we didn't even know were there!

. . . .

Once unknown expectations become known, what do we do with them? How do we keep these puppies from causing unnecessary conflict in our marriage? We apply our God-tool of acceptance. We accept our spouse's differences, resisting the urge to determine they are wrong. We recognize there is more than "our way" of doing things and that both ways are okay. Like my friend Rhonda says, 2+2=4, but so does 3+1 and 4+0. Rhonda used math to come to grips with her unknown expectations in the early years of marriage when she was working a full-time job with lots of travel and much of the house and childcare responsibilities were falling on her husband. He shopped differently than she did. He managed the house differently than she would. He cared for their daughter differently than she would. Yet, the shopping, managing the household, and caring for their daughter were still accomplished. Sometimes we forget there's more than one way to accomplish the same thing.

Humility is an important part of dealing with unknown expectations. The opposite of humility is pride, and it can so easily slip into our thinking with expectations. "My way is the right way" is prideful thinking. Humility says, "Your way is just as valuable as my way and it's okay for us to be different." Notice we didn't say "Your way is just as good as my way." Why is that important? We're so glad you asked.

One partner in the marriage is likely more focused on efficiency than the other. In our marriage, that's Jill, not me. I drive without giving much thought to how I will get there. I cook without having "the big picture" in mind. Actually, I do think through details and I do plan, but I think more in "chunks" that are in no particular order rather than in lists. I also tend to be more impulsive — or spur of the moment — than planned.

Of course, this drives me (Jill) absolutely nuts! My thinking is very sequential. I think through the details of a project, assembling everything I need before starting. I drive somewhere very strategically, thinking about traffic and what route is the most direct. I check to make sure I have all my ingredients before I cook. In my mind, there's a logical step-by-step approach to anything you do.

Several years ago, Mark and I learned about something called "mind styles." Based upon the research of Anthony Gregorc, there are four different kinds of "thinking/processing styles": concrete sequential, concrete random, abstract sequential, and abstract random.[5] This was very enlightening for our marriage, as we discovered how our minds are created differently. Your mind style is either concrete or abstract and either random or sequential. Let's spend a few minutes learning about the four different mind styles to see if you can see yourself or your spouse in this.

Your Mind's Perception Ability

Concrete: This quality allows you to gather information directly through your five senses: sight, smell, touch, taste, and hearing. When you are using your concrete ability, you are dealing with the obvious, the "here and now," the facts, and are not looking for hidden meanings or making connections between ideas or concepts.

Abstract: This quality allows you to visualize, imagine, conceive ideas, to understand or believe that which you can't really see. When you are using your abstract quality, you use intuition, imagination, and you are looking beyond "what is" to the hidden meaning and connections.

. . . .

We all have the ability to perceive in concrete and abstract ways to some extent, but most of us are more inclined to use one more than the other. A natural concrete thinker will often communicate in a very direct, literal, no-nonsense manner, while a natural abstract thinker may use subtle methods such as metaphor to get the same meaning. Conversations between these two thinking styles may have a lot of misunderstanding.

In our marriage, Jill's the concrete thinker and I'm the abstract thinker. Jill's direct, no-nonsense communication used to feel abrasive to me. However, once I understood that was a result of how her brain works and how God made her, I stopped taking her forthrightness so personally.

Mark often "sees" things I (Jill) don't see. For instance, one evening after dinner, Mark mentioned that one of our kids was really quiet at the dinner table. "Do you think he's struggling with something?" Mark asked. My response (true to my concrete mind style!) was, "Hmmm . . . I don't know. He didn't say anything, so I think he's fine."

Your Mind's Ordering Ability

Sequential: Your mind organizes information in a **linear**, step-by-step manner. When you use sequential ability, you follow a logical train of thought and may also have a plan to follow rather than relying on impulse.

Random: Lets your mind organize information by **chunks**, and in no particular order. When you use random ability, you can skip steps in a procedure and still produce the result or outcome you want. You may even start in the middle, or at the end, and work backward. You may like life to be more impulsive or spur-of-the-moment than planned.

We all have ability in both ways of ordering, but usually we tend to use one more easily and comfortably than the other. In our marriage, I (Jill) am sequential and Mark is random. This can certainly cause its challenges in marriage. My logical, sequential brain doesn't understand how Mark's random brain works. Of course, Mark's random brain wants my sequential brain to relax a little, think outside the box, and not get upset when things aren't done in a certain order.

Are you wondering how we wrote a book together without killing each other?

Simply knowing about these differences can be a game changer in marriage. If we don't know about them, thinking styles become an unknown expectation that often wreaks havoc in marriage. We expect our spouse to think the same way we do, and most likely, they do not! God created each of our brains to process life and make decisions in a unique way. This is news to many of us who have been trying for entirely too long to change our spouse to be more like we are. Today is the day to make an acquaintance with your unknown expectations and begin to accept your spouse rather than criticizing him or her.

Are you wondering how we wrote a book together without killing each other? Mark took the topics in the book and wrote his "random" thoughts, stories, and perspectives on them. I then took his random thoughts and put them in a sequential order in the book. Ten years ago when we wrote our book *Living with Less So Your Family Has More*, we didn't know about our differing mind styles. Suffice it to say that we didn't work nearly as well together on that project. Understanding each other and accepting our differing ways has made a huge difference in our ability to work together—whether it's in everyday life or writing a book together!

The best way to handle unknown expectations is to examine the assumptions you've made about how your spouse should think, do, or respond. Dig deep and honestly evaluate if you've been prideful in believing your way is the right way, the only way, or the best way. Squash that pride once and for all and accept the reality that your spouse is different than you.

UNSPOKEN EXPECTATIONS

In our nearly thirty years of ministry, we've spent many hours sitting across from hundreds of married couples in crisis. As we help them untangle the mess in their marriage, usually they communicate their disappointment that marriage isn't what they thought it would be or their spouse doesn't do what they want them to do.

Particularly when I'm (Mark) meeting with the husband or when Jill is meeting one-on-one with the wife, they will open up about how they are disappointed with their spouse. We will often ask, "Have you told him you long for that?" or "Have you told her you expect that?" The answer is often, "No. I haven't." Sometimes that answer is followed up with, "I don't think I should have to." This turns unspoken expectations into unrealistic expectations, which eventually become unmet expectations. It's a slippery slope for sure.

Unfortunately, unspoken expectations are rarely verbalized in a

. . . .

healthy way. They usually are spewed out in an argument, which, if you haven't figured it out yet, is an ineffective time to communicate. The best way to identify unspoken expectations is to ask yourself these two questions:

What do I long for from my spouse?

What do I expect, but feel I shouldn't have to tell my spouse?

The best way to disassemble unspoken expectations is with honest conversation outside of conflict. A great way to start that conversation is by saying, "I'm realizing that I've expected things from you that I've never mentioned before. It's unfair of me to be frustrated with you for not fulfilling my desires when you don't even know they exist! I'd like to share the things I'm realizing I need so maybe we can talk through them." Communicating your expectations doesn't give a full assurance that your desires will be fulfilled, but it is the first step to stop bitterness and perceived offense before they put more of a wedge in your relationship.

UNREALISTIC EXPECTATIONS

Moving into marriage, I (Mark) had the following expectations.

Sex would be great.
We would have similar interests.
Sex would be anytime anywhere.
We would be soulmates.
We would always be in love and express love.
Sex would be fabulous.
We would never fight or argue.

We would be best friends.
Sex would happen often.
We would live in a love story.

Like many guys, I was introduced to pornography somewhere around junior high. The pictures were tantalizing for the eyes but the articles were enticing for the heart, and captivating for my mind. They painted a picture that women want sex anytime anyplace. They also communicated that women were adventuresome sexually. By the time I married ten years later, I'd consumed enough false messages about sex that my expectations were off the charts. There was no winning on Jill's part. Sex was never frequent enough, good enough, or adventuresome enough for me because of my unrealistic expectations.

Moving into marriage, I (Jill) had these expectations:

My husband would be a strong leader.
We would laugh and have fun together.
We would talk and make decisions together.
My husband would be romantic, often surprising me with his
    thoughtfulness.
We would build a family together and parent well together.
We would be best friends.
We would grow together in our faith.
We would never fight or argue (because I never saw my
    parents disagree).
We would think alike.
We would have an incredible love story.

. . . .

Like many girls, I had consumed my fair share of romance novels, chick flicks, and magazine articles that filled my head with all kinds of messages about marriage, romance, and being in love. Notice that sex wasn't even on the list. Oh, I assumed sex would just happen and not be an issue, but it didn't make my top ten list of expectations. Looking at both of our lists of expectations, is it any wonder we ended up in a marriage counselor's office?

As I (Mark) look back, I understand now that I had little positive influence in my life on marriage. I had never witnessed a good marriage. I didn't attend church growing up. I didn't have good role models in my life. I had huge gaps when it came to relationships. Again, I didn't know what I didn't know.

Jill and I were invited, early on in our marriage, to attend a marriage retreat. I initially thought that was a great idea. Right away reality hit, though, and it hit hard. At the retreat, Jill began to cry and continued to cry throughout the retreat. I had no idea what was happening. I didn't know anything was wrong in our marriage. It was there that I learned that our marriage was not perfect, needed work, and that we were beginning a journey of marriage discovery that would be a lifelong adventure.

I wish I could say that I put unrealistic expectations to bed for good that weekend. We uncovered some pain points in our relationship and began to talk about important things, but I still believed deep down that marriage shouldn't be this hard, and I entertained the thought that maybe we really weren't made for each other. Remember how fades start? Yep, just one centimeter off center. My inclination to look outside my marriage started years before when I invited my unrealistic expectations home for dinner. I entertained them deep in my heart,

. . . .

never revealing what I was thinking, but believing it more and more all the time. The lie was brewing a bitterness deep within my soul. This was the beginning of my fade that started with disappointments, moved to discouragement, and eventually expanded into disillusionment.

Unrealistic expectations also show up when we idealistically believe that our spouse will see things the way we see things. This happens to me (Jill) when it comes to things around the house. When I put something on the steps to be moved from the downstairs to the upstairs, it seems I'm the only one who sees it there. Mark's unbothered by clutter on the kitchen counters and will leave things there for weeks unless I ask him to put them away. It's as if he cannot see them. The truth is he doesn't see them like I do, and as long as I expect him to, my expectations are unrealistic. My priorities are not his priorities. What's important to me isn't what's important to him (see more about this in the next chapter). If I need his help in keeping the kitchen counters or the steps cleaned off, I have to *ask* him, not expect him to (literally) see things the way I do.

Unrealistic expectations are where the Perfection Infection shows up in our marriage. Remember, the Perfection Infection is when we have unrealistic expectations of ourselves and of others, and when we unfairly compare ourselves and others. Most of our expectations and comparisons show up because we've idolized other marriage relationships (e.g., my parents never had conflict, we won't either), we've allowed the media to feed us lies of impossible standards (e.g., relationships should be as easy as *People* magazine makes them appear), or we've concocted our own unreasonable ideals (we're so in love we'll never have issues).

....

What do we do with these crazy, unrealistic expectations that are robbing us of our joy and causing distance in our relationship? We start by identifying exactly what expectations we have and examining them to understand why they're unrealistic. Are they from our family of origin? Previous relationships or a previous marriage? Our own idealism? The culture? Unreasonable beliefs? Once we identify those unrealistic expectations, we replace them with reality. More on that in a moment.

> *When what we expect doesn't match up to what we have, we're not sure what to do about it.*

UNMET EXPECTATIONS

Our years of mentoring hurting couples and dealing with our own hurting relationship have caused us to conclude that the number one cause of divorce isn't money, sex, infidelity, or communication. Those are secondary issues of a deeper issue. They are symptoms of the root issue of unmet expectations. When what we expect doesn't match up to what we have, we're not sure what to do with it. We usually respond in one of two ways: (1) we respond with anger demanding that our relationship become what we want or (2) we squelch our disappointment, pushing it deep inside, telling ourselves "it doesn't matter," when really it does. Neither response is healthy or helpful for our relationship. So what is?

Most of our conversation about expectations has focused on how dangerous they are. And indeed they are, especially if they are unknown, unspoken, or unrealistic. However, expectations can also be a good thing if we learn how to identify them, communicate about them, and use them to strengthen and improve our relationship. Let's look at how we can stop the slow fade of unmet expectations and how to use them to benefit our perfectly imperfect marriage.

Learn to Accept Rather Than Expect

This is particularly important when you're dealing with differing ways of thinking, processing, and making decisions. In the past I (Mark) was so disappointed with Jill and our differences, I held her hostage to them. I was blaming, attacking, and condemning her for things that were not wrong, just different. I was brewing a bitterness within me that was entrapping my soul. I was leaving my marriage emotionally before I ever left it physically.

With my heart relinquished fully to God, I now handle our differences very differently. I'm no longer fighting them. In fact, now I try to find the good and the opportunity in our differences. I'm loving the real, not the dream. I'm now understanding that it takes both of our perspectives to see an accurate picture and the full scope of whatever opportunity is in front of us.

Replace the Lies of Expectations with the Truth of Reality

Here are some reality statements every married person needs to accept:

You will likely "bump into" each other's differences for the duration of your marriage. If you leave this marriage and head into another marriage, it will take you about two years to start bumping into differences in that new marriage. It's the nature of living in relationship with another person. These days I (Mark) am keeping my idealism better balanced. I know I'm a dreamer and always will be, but I work to keep those dreams evened out with realism. My experience taught me that the grass isn't really greener on the other side of the fence—there are just different weeds over there! My focus is to stay steady with my God and to not waver in any manner.

When you bump into your spouse's differences, you will likely have to deal with judgment in your own heart. These days I (Jill) am keeping my mouth shut a lot more than I ever have. Don't get me wrong, I'm not shoving things under the carpet that need to be addressed. I'm simply addressing less, keeping my thoughts and comments to myself, letting Mark be Mark and Jill be Jill. I'm applying Proverbs 21:23 (ESV), "Whoever keeps his mouth and his tongue keeps himself out of trouble," and Ephesians 4:29 (ESV), "Let no corrupting talk come out of your mouths, but only such as is good for building up . . . that it may give grace to those who hear." I'm also resisting the temptation to present counter requests for change. I've learned that "I'll work on that if you agree to work on _____" is never a healthy response.

You will likely not understand all your spouse's concerns, but you still have to value them. You don't get to *decide* what's important to your spouse. You do, however, get to *discover* what's important to him or her. I (Jill) am listening more intently and not taking things at face value. I'm listening for Mark's emotions behind his words. I'm asking more questions or encouraging more conversation by using phrases like, "Tell me more," or "How can I help?" These phrases show genuine concern.

Don't Fertilize Fault-Finding Thoughts

Most of us need to do both internal work and external work in our marriage. Evaluating our thought life is important internal work because what we feed will grow. We can actually push our thoughts in the right direction if we will starve the negative thoughts and feed the positive thoughts. Start paying attention to your thoughts about your spouse. When a negative thought enters your mind, flip it on its head. Turn the negative thought into a positive one. For instance, one friend I (Jill) was talking with was frustrated when her husband decided to cut their boys' hair the morning they were trying to get out the door for a trip. I challenged her to reframe her frustration and be grateful she had a husband who took initiative to cut their sons' hair.

Use Expectations as a Springboard for Healthy Conversations

Tell your spouse that you've identified some expectations you have and you want to talk through them. Own the fact that these have been unspoken and maybe even unknown. Tell your spouse you want to sort out if these are unrealistic expectations or real desires that could possibly be a part of the fabric of your relationship if you simply communicated them.

When you desire something different in your marriage, it's okay to talk with your spouse about your yearning. It's okay to ask for change but not expect it. Your spouse may be overwhelmed or not feel led to work on that aspect of themselves in your time frame. We have to allow the Holy Spirit to lead after we ask or create awareness. Be ready, however, to make some changes yourself, because you'll likely need to meet in the middle in some way. For instance, when I asked Mark to be more of a leader in our home, the conversation started with us talking about his passivity, but it moved to talking about my tendency to consistently challenge his leadership. I had to own the fact that as much as I desired him to lead, I often undermined his leadership when he did lead. He had to own his passivity and I had to own my tendency to control.

In the past I (Mark) threw my disappointment and discouragement out there in frustration. I didn't know how to engage them any differently, but now I'm doing the internal work to manage my thought life and the external work to pursue honest communication.

Expect the Right Things

Some expectations can be helpful for marriage. These are things that will happen in every marriage. Once you say, "I do," it's healthy to:

Expect Conflict: You are two different human beings with differing personalities, temperaments, opinions, and preferences. Conflict will happen.

Expect Disappointments: Your spouse will make mistakes. He or she will let you down. They are not perfect and disappointment will happen.

Expect to Be Annoyed: When you live in close proximity to someone else as you do in marriage, there will be things that annoy you. In fact, the very things that drew you to each other in the first place will often be the things that will annoy you later on because they are the things that are different from you.

Expect to Need Continuing Education: Marriage requires a lifetime of learning. In order to have a deepening intimacy that lasts a lifetime, you'll need to keep learning about yourself, your spouse, God, and marriage.

Expect to Overcommunicate: Your spouse can't read your mind. They have their own balls to juggle in life. You'll need to work hard to make sure you listen well and communicate clearly.

Expect to Lose That Loving Feeling: Feelings will wane, and that's a normal part of a lifelong relationship. Feelings of love and attraction will come and go. There will be seasons where you'll have to choose to love because the feeling just won't be there.

Expect to Keep Investing: Your marriage relationship will need to be invested in on a regular basis. You'll have to continue to date, to flirt, to communicate, to learn, to play together, to spend time, to listen well, and to have fun together.

Expect to Ask for Help: It's very possible that there may be times where you need to seek accountability or perspective or help from a mentor, another couple, or a professional counselor to get through a tough season. Asking for help is a sign of strength. (Clue: if you are often considering leaving or are disconnecting emotionally from your spouse or go days after conflict without interacting, these symptoms are signs that you are struggling with creating change on your own and need to pursue wise counsel.)

Use the Right Tools for the Job

Humility, courage, grace, and acceptance are likely the best tools to pull out of your toolbox when you're doing marriage improvement work in the area of expectations. **Humility** will offset pride that says

....

my way is the right way. **Courage** is needed to have honest conversations when they are desperately needed. **Grace** needs to permeate your heart, allowing your spouse to be imperfect. **Acceptance** will allow you to resist the urge to change your spouse when it comes to things that are simply different. There are enough changes that will need to be made as marriage brings about maturity without requiring changes on issues we simply need to accept.

⊹ **THINK ABOUT IT** ⊹

Where do you have unrealistic expectations in your marriage? How do you need to adjust your expectations to better match reality? Do you need to ask for some honest conversation with your spouse? Are unrealistic expectations the start of a slow fade in your marriage? If so, you can begin to turn that around today!

⊹ **TALK ABOUT IT** ⊹

My biggest takeaway from this chapter was _____
_____

I've never given it much thought, but I have had these unknown expectations: _____
_____

After reading this chapter, I realize that I have these unspoken expectations: _____
_____

....

⚜ TALK TO GOD ABOUT IT ⚜

Lord, thank You for this opportunity to learn. Help me to take the words on these pages and apply them practically to my life. Reveal my unknown expectations. Help me identify my unspoken hopes and to have the courage to talk about them with my spouse. Help me to stop any fade in my heart that has to do with unmet expectations. Lord, lead me to accept more than I expect. In Jesus' Name. Amen.

Today's Truth: "[Do] not give the devil a foothold."
EPHESIANS 4:27

. . . .

## CHAPTER 5

IF IT MATTERS TO *Me* IT SHOULD MATTER TO *You*

THE SLOW FADE OF MINIMIZING

Now that we're nearing the empty nest, we've enjoyed going to a 7 a.m. kickboxing class almost every weekday morning. On one morning when we had a new instructor, Mark and I had to leave the class fifteen minutes early so I could be on time for a meeting. We sprayed down our boxing bag, put it away, and headed out the door as the class continued. The next day one of our classmates said to us, "After class yesterday, the instructor wondered aloud if 'that couple who left didn't like her teaching.'" He said he reassured her that we probably had somewhere to be.

. . . .

As Mark and I processed that conversation, we marveled at that instructor's instinct to make our exit about her. Because we were in the middle of writing this book and were running everything through the lens of marriage, I blurted, "So can you imagine being married to that?"

Mark thoughtfully responded, "You are."

Insecurity. It dogs many of us. And it's fodder for the slow fade of minimizing. Here's our story:

Mark: The word *minimize* means to "treat something as less important than it really is." I did this for many years in our marriage. Something would happen and I'd just let it slide. The only problem is that it wasn't sliding. It was pooling. It was accumulating in my head and my heart, fading from minimizing to harboring, and eventually to bitterness.

When we decide to allow another person to be different from us, we give them the space to be themselves.

Jill: I had no idea of the cesspool of emotions Mark had churning inside of him. Occasionally he would express frustration at something, and that's where my minimizing came into play. I would minimize his frustration. I didn't dig deeper, I didn't ask questions; I just gave him a logical response that made sense to me—the thinker—but didn't tend to his—the feeler's—emotions.

Mark: There is a healthy side to letting things go. When we decide to allow another person to be different from us, we give them the space to be themselves. When we decide not to address every little thing our spouse does wrong, we give them "grace" to be imperfect. Every relationship needs space and grace—some of that give-and-take—or we'd be dealing with conflict all of the time.

What happens with minimizing is that something that needs to be addressed is instead buried. We tell ourselves things like, "It doesn't matter." "It will never change." "It's not worth the conflict." When we do this, we miss the opportunity to figure something out together, strengthen our relationship, and deepen our intimacy.

Jill: Minimizing keeps real issues buried beneath the surface, unaddressed, untended, simmering in the darkness of our heart. When we keep something in the dark, it becomes the enemy's playground. In fact, that's how marriage fades happen. We begin with real feelings and real responses to everyday life. Instead of attending to those feelings in a healthy manner that would move us closer to each other, we too often choose to stuff the feelings, building up walls in our heart we don't even realize are there.

Mark: There is a spiritual battle going on for every marriage. The Bible tells us that Satan's goal is to steal and destroy (John 10:10). Your spouse is not your enemy, but Satan will do his best to convince you that he or she is. The Bible calls Satan the "father of lies" because that's how he does his convincing. He works in the dark places of our heart, whispering lies about us and our spouse, taking ground and creating distance in our marriage without us even realizing it.

WHAT KIND OF MINIMIZER ARE YOU?

There are two kinds of minimizers found in most marriages: internal and external. Internal minimizers are those who minimize their own feelings and concerns. External minimizers are those who minimize the feelings and concerns of their spouse. Both of these kick minimizing into gear, pulling us away from each other.

In our marriage, I (Mark) tend to be the *internal* minimizer. There's no doubt in my mind that my self-minimizing came primarily from my home of origin. Growing up in a broken home with an abusive stepfather, my feelings were minimized and rarely considered. I did whatever I could to keep the peace, so I learned early on to tell myself minimizing messages like, "It's not a big deal," or "Just let it go," or "It doesn't matter." My people-pleasing set in at an early age.

Temperament can figure into minimizing as well. I naturally have a servant heart. Always have. There's a positive side of serving and even pleasing people that comes out of care and compassion. I'm very tuned in to other people's pain and sensitive to their needs. However, when I become consumed with what others think, my people-pleasing moves into an unhealthy place. Fueled by my insecurities, this is when I tend to minimize my feelings, thoughts, and concerns.

If I don't do anything about it, my minimizing will eventually turn into harboring as I tuck away the "injustice" of my untended hurts deep in my heart. Fueled by insecurity, I harbor my hurt. What I don't realize is that I'm actually the one doing the denying because Jill can't possibly know about my feelings, thoughts, or concerns if I don't value them and express them to her. Untended, minimizing too easily moves from harboring into bitterness. By this time I've put a lot of distance between my heart and Jill's heart. I've separated us inside my head.

When we get in the habit of swallowing our feelings and turning against our partner rather than stating how we feel, we're in dangerous territory. If you tend to be an internal minimizer like Mark, you have to begin using your God-tool of courage. You need courage to speak up, preferably in times when you are not in the midst of conflict. You need to raise the importance of your thoughts and concerns, putting them on an equal status with the thoughts and concerns your spouse communicates.

Too often internal minimizers only put themselves out there in crisis. For instance, I (Mark) only spoke up when I was fed up and reacted in anger. Unfortunately this is the least likely place to be heard. Emotions are high and communication is compromised. So when all seems peaceful but you need to bring up an issue or concern, that is the time to speak up, as hard as it seems.

Yes, you will have to face your fear of inciting conflict. You may even experience more conflict as you raise your thoughts and concerns to a new level, throwing off the established patterns in your marriage.

It might even be good to have a "this is what I'm learning about myself" chat with your spouse, letting him or her know that you're recognizing that you tend to be an internal minimizer and you're realizing it's not healthy for you or your marriage, so you'll be stepping up in courage to put your thoughts and feelings on the table both inside and outside of conflict.

Another way to have conversations is to "ask your thoughts." The other morning, Jill was coming off as frustrated and irritated. She was somewhat aggressive in her tone and interaction. Instead of feeding my negative thoughts about our interaction, I decided to actually ask her, "Are you okay? You seem frustrated and irritated." She responded she was under a great deal of tension regarding the ministry she leads and apologized for her irritability.

In our marriage, I (Jill) tend to be the *external* minimizer. Much of my minimizing comes from my tendency to disregard feelings in general. Like Mark, this comes also from a blend of my family of origin mixed with my temperament and personality. Growing up, my family didn't do a lot with feelings. When difficulties surfaced, we exuded strength and simply "bucked up" and got to the other side of hard. This experience has honestly served me well to lead through tough situations in the ministry and work world, but it hasn't particularly served me well as a wife and mother. My tendency to minimize my own feelings (yes, I do my own internal minimizing when it comes to feelings) was unwittingly leading me to sometimes minimize others' feelings as well.

Because of this, one place I've asked God to grow me is in understanding and embracing my own feelings. Instead of defaulting into buck-up mode, I'm tuning in to what I'm feeling, talking to God about those feelings, allowing Jesus—who experienced every feeling we feel—to minister to my heart before moving into solution mode.

When Mark's depression and anxiety threaten to put a rain cloud over his personal sunshine, too often I want to tell him it isn't really cloudy and he simply needs to push the clouds aside to see the sunshine that's there. It's a perfectly logical response from someone who's never experienced depression or anxiety, but it isn't what he needs. He needs validation. This is where I also need courage, but from a slightly different angle.

Validation confirms that other people can have their own emotional experience, and it is likely different than yours. This is desperately needed in marriage because we're each wired uniquely as individuals. We have to have the courage to let our spouse live through his or her own emotional experience even if we don't understand it ourselves. It's not necessarily agreeing with their feelings, it's simply recognizing the reality of how they are feeling. The beautiful part of validation is that it can actually grow us closer together. When we allow them to share their feelings and let go of emotion, we're able to know our spouse's heart more.

COURAGE, COMPASSION, AND VALIDATING

Minimizing can occur when we enter into unknown emotional territory, and our human nature wants to shut it down rather than draw it out. This is where we need **courage** to do the opposite of what we feel and **compassion** to respond with validating statements that are gentle and empathetic, like:

- "It seems to me that you felt disrespected in this situation."
- "Does it feel like you've been blindsided?"
- "It must be very difficult to be in this situation."
- "I can't even begin to imagine what you are feeling."
- "I'm sensing that this brought up real feelings of betrayal."
- "Tell me if I have it right. What I heard you say was my statement was very hurtful toward you and it is not the first time you have felt this way."
- "Let me make sure I'm hearing you correctly. You feel like you don't matter, your feelings don't matter, and you are feeling resentful. Is that right?"

The key to validating is using words or phrases that explore what the other is experiencing. Once you make a statement of validation, it's important to stop and listen to what the person says next and then try to help substantiate those feelings. Continue this back-and-forth process

The most beautiful gift you can give your spouse is letting them feel understood without you ever actually saying, "I understand."

until the person feels understood.

Ironically, saying to someone "I understand" is typically not helpful and actually tends to minimize their feelings. Instead, the most beautiful gift you can give your spouse is letting them *feel* understood by confirming and validating their emotions without ever actually saying the words.

Are you a fixer like I am? Do you feel like validating is just delaying the inevitable need to fix the problem? Here's what I've learned: validating is part of compassion, and it helps my husband gain the emotional and spiritual strength he needs to deal with the challenge before him. It reassures him he's not alone; it puts a sense of calm and peace into the picture; and, if needed, opens him up to receiving help. In other words, validating helps him to move from feeling to fixing. We arrive at the same endpoint, but we take a different road to get us there. It might not feel like the most efficient route, but I can assure you it is the most efficient route for someone who has strong feelings. For those of us who are natural fixers, this is important to know and understand!

Compassion nurtures emotional safety, and when people feel emotionally safe, they share more. When they share more, we learn more, connect better, and are able to deepen intimacy. This helps provide support in a nonthreatening way that will more likely get to the root of the problem.

SLOW THE PACE; GIVE LOVE SPACE

Did you just read the previous section about validating and think to yourself, *You've got to be kidding me! I don't have time for that!* Many of us do, particularly Type A, driven, high-capacity get-it-done folks. The truth is, relationships take time. In order to tune in to, connect with, and really have intimacy with another person we need to slow down enough to have deeper conversations. Marriage requires us to down-shift more often than many of us realize.

When I (Jill) find myself slipping back into minimizing, it almost always happens when the calendar is full and there's little margin in life. I'm spinning my plates like my high-capacity self can do so well, but I'm touching each plate less often. Relationships that really matter can't be tossed, but instead must be held. This requires us to slow our pace and give relationships the space they need and deserve.

The truth is, for many of us who like to run at a faster speed, we're *more comfortable doing than being.* We may tell ourselves that feelings only complicate things and are useless in accomplishing anything worthwhile. This "lie of doing," based on our own version of insecurity, keeps us treading water instead of lying on the beach enjoying the sun. It keeps us focused on projects instead of people. It keeps us striving instead of thriving.

Drive-through relationships are just as unhealthy as drive-through food.

When life is moving faster than is healthy for our relationships, it's easy to minimize, both internally and externally. We internally minimize when we say to ourselves, "I don't have the time or energy to deal with this," or "She doesn't have time for me," or "He doesn't care." This kind of self-talk puts distance between us and our spouse. It erodes intimacy and pulls us apart when we need to be drawing closer. Drive-through relationships are just as unhealthy as drive-through food.

So how do you tune out the world and tune in to your marriage?

Here are six practical ways to increase margin and decrease minimizing:

Eat dinner around the table. Make dinner prep something you do as a couple. Then linger at the table and talk (if you don't have little ones pulling you away!). Make mealtime as much about relationship as it is about food.

Put away your screens. Determine where and when screens are fine and where they need to be tucked away or turned off. Mealtime. Conversations. Vacation. Date night. These are all places where our screens need to be put away. Will this take some self-control? Probably. Will doing so communicate value to your loved ones? Absolutely. It will also increase your patience and decrease your temptation to minimize.

Stop. Look. Listen. We use these three words to teach our kids how to cross the street. We also need to use them to teach ourselves how to cross into our spouse's world. When your loved one enters into your space, *stop* what you're doing. Close the computer. Pause the television or video game. Walk away from your task to warmly greet him or her. *Look* at him or her fully. Maintain eye contact. Then *listen* with your eyes and your ears. Listen to learn. To hear his question. To understand her feelings.

Talk to God together. This may feel awkward at first if you're not accustomed to praying together, but prayer always slows down our pace and gives us opportunity to hear what is weighing heavy on our partner's mind. Now that we're almost empty nesters, Jill and I often pray in the car when we're driving somewhere. When the kids were smaller, we would try to pray at night as we crawled into bed; however, we often found one or both of us slipping off to sleep sooner rather than later.

Some couples find praying together after making love works well for them, thanking God for their marriage, their love, and lifting up whatever is on their heart and mind. If your spouse refuses to pray with you, you can still reach out and hold hands and silently pray for both of you.

Connect and catch up. If you have little ones, take some time to talk after the kids are in bed. Are you empty nesters? You still have to be intentional about setting aside time to connect. In the summer, enjoy the porch together. In the winter, resist the urge to flip on the television or hop on the computer until you've taken some time to connect and catch up. Take a few minutes to ask questions like, "What was the best part of your day?" or "What was the hardest part of your day?" or "What's bothering you the most and how can I help you?" or "What's weighing heavy on you today?" or "How can I be praying for you?" These connecting questions help us maximize interest.

Date your mate. Dating your mate means bringing your best self fully present for a specified period of time just as you did when you were single and trying to impress the person you were interested in. Life is busy, so you have to set aside space in your days, weeks, and months to nurture your marriage. Create a repeating schedule you both prioritize for time together. Sometimes that may be as simple as the first thirty minutes after the kids are in bed. Ideally, it is once a week or once every other week or, at a minimum, once a month where you get a sitter/let the kids go to grandma's/trade sitting with another couple and enjoy some focused time without interruptions. Even if you're empty nesters, date night is important because you're getting away from the everyday routine and focusing on each other. Slowing down and taking time to relate is essential in sustaining intimacy.

....

Jill: As you can see, the primary tool to turn minimizing around is **courage**. Courage to be honest. Courage to dig deeply. Courage to ask questions. Courage to hear real answers to those questions. Along with courage, you need **compassion** and **love** as well.

Mark: These days I'm bringing thoughts and feelings to the table before they take up residence in my heart. When I feel like Jill's tone of voice is condescending or belittling, I'm resisting the urge to internally minimize and instead addressing it in the moment. When I don't feel like she's listening to me, I'm asking for her full attention. If I feel disrespected, I'm letting her know that I feel that way rather than harboring that in my heart and providing fertilizer for bitterness.

She's making it safe for me to do that, too. She's dialed down defensiveness so that when I bring something to the table she's receiving my feedback and apologizing when needed. We're not doing it perfectly, but it's a great improvement from our past history of minimizing.

Jill: These days I'm tuning in to my own emotions. I'm also working to keep a short leash on thoughts and feelings. I've learned that when I bring them to the table, they no longer have a hold on me. When I feel unloved because of something Mark has said or done, I'm letting him know. Often those things aren't intentional, but they are still very real.

When Mark expresses frustration, I'm working to not minimize his perspective, but rather to acknowledge it and give it value with validating responses. I'm asking more questions—seeking to understand rather than disagree.

Mark: Contrary to popular belief, we can't coast in marriage. We have to keep learning, growing, and changing. We have to allow God to mold and change us to be more like Jesus each and every day.

. . . .

Jill: If you are reading this and see yourself in our descriptions of "minimizing" your spouse's expressed concerns, you need courage to dig deeper. Resist the urge to dismiss your spouse's concern or explain them away. Tend to their feelings, show compassion, and ask questions to understand. You don't have to agree to understand. There's plenty of time to disagree or share your thoughts. For now, just let them know they've been heard and their concerns are important.

Mark: If your spouse really has trouble hearing you or you feel they are minimizing your concerns, you may have to have the courage to ask for help. We have found marriage counseling to be helpful in those times. If your spouse is unwilling to go, then go by yourself. You'll still benefit from having someone help you understand what you bring to the marriage table and it may actually open the door for your spouse to join you at some point. (Note: if you start with a counselor for a long period of time, it's considered unethical in the counseling profession to add your spouse. The individual counseling can help you work on your ability to connect, communicate, and respond to your spouse. Hopefully, your spouse will see your commitment to change and it will open the door for the two of you to begin marriage counseling together with another counselor.)

Jill: Pay attention to how much minimizing is going on in your marriage. As much as it depends upon you, take steps to stop this slow fade before any more ground is taken.

❧ THINK ABOUT IT ❧

Are you minimizing your spouse's concerns? Are you minimizing your own concerns? Are you fading from minimizing into harboring hurt or even bitterness? Where do you need to have courage in your marriage?

❧ TALK ABOUT IT ❧

My biggest takeaway from this chapter was_____
_____

I've never given it much thought, but I can see that I minimize
_____

_____

After reading this chapter, I realize that I most need to use my God-tool of _____

_____

❧ TALK TO GOD ABOUT IT ❧

Lord, thank You for helping me to see things I've never seen before. Help me to stop minimizing. Reveal any internal minimizing I'm doing and help me to understand where I learned to minimize my concerns and feelings. Help me to have the courage to have conversations I'd rather not have. Show me any ways I minimize _____'s feelings. Give me the courage to ask questions, validate, and step into his/her world. And, Lord, we need to slow down and take time for each other. Show me how to practically make that happen. In Jesus' Name. Amen.

Today's Truth: "Let all bitterness and wrath and anger and clamor and slander be put away from you, along with all malice. Be kind to one another, tenderhearted, forgiving one another, as God in Christ forgave you." EPHESIANS 4:31–32 (ESV)

## CHAPTER 6

WHEN I SAID "*I Do*," I DIDN'T MEAN *That!*

THE SLOW FADE OF NOT ACCEPTING

Nana, look at this bug!" "Pappaw, see the clouds . . . they look like a dog!" "Nana, push me higher—I want to see how my tummy feels." "Pappaw, look at these ants—they're so tiny!"

These are all statements that have been uttered at our home recently as we interact with our grandkids. As they learn about their world, there is such a sense of discovery in kids!

Marriage requires the same sense of discovery. It's inside each of us, but buried beneath the responsibilities and stresses of everyday life. Too often we forget about discovery and declare, "We're incompatible!"

· · · · · · · ·

The truth is we're all wonderfully incompatible, and marriage simply brings a magnifying glass to those differences. If we don't learn to accept one another, distance grows in our relationship. If not addressed, this fade can end up at rejection, which puts miles between our hearts.

Instead of being frustrated with each other's personalities and temperaments, we have to learn to be fascinated by the differences! That move from frustration to fascination can only happen when we unbury our sense of discovery. Here's our story:

Jill: For most of us, our spouse's differences are what drew us to one another in the first place. It's not until we say "I do" and begin to live every day together that those same differences begin to grate on our nerves.

Too often I felt like her strength came across as parenting me.

Mark: I was drawn to Jill's strength when we first met. She knew what she wanted and she went after it. She was sure of herself. And most importantly, she was a believer. After receiving Christ, I knew I wanted to marry a Christian woman. Jill was strong in her faith.

After we got married, however, I grew to dislike her strength. When she believed in something, she strongly believed in something. She was black and white and I had a little more gray in me. She was organized, knowledgeable, and a strong leader. But too often I felt like her strength came across as parenting me. Sometimes it was *what* she said and sometimes it was *how* she said something.

Jill: Mark was tender, easygoing, and compassionate. He was funny, friendly, and the life of the party. After we got married, his extrovert-self clashed with my introvert-self. His easygoing spirit allowed for far more "gray" than I was comfortable with.

Mark is a "feeler." I loved that when it meant he was tender, compassionate, and romantic. I disliked it when he based decisions on feeling rather than thinking, which was how I made decisions. He also wanted to touch all the time. I, on the other hand, really like my personal space.

Mark: I wasn't aware of it at the time, but in retrospect, my fade moved from not accepting our differences to wanting her to change. Our disagreements were often fueled by my attempt to force her to change. When this didn't work, I moved to the place of rejection.

I'm grateful for how God has redeemed the brokenness I created in our family, but I now know that my determination that we were just "too incompatible" was a lie from the enemy that I believed hook, line, and sinker.

Jill: In fact, it was our differences that caused Mark to shut down on our Florida trip. We had been sitting on the beach reading. Mark kept wanting to hold my hand. The constant need to be touching was driving me crazy and I said in frustration, "I'm not going anywhere. I'm right here beside you. We don't have to be touching all the time."

Mark: The minute she said that, I determined I was done with our differences. I moved from trying to change her to rejecting her. It never crossed my mind that there could be a middle ground in me honoring her need for space, in the midst of seeking to have my need for touch met.

Not only that, but I took Jill's need for space as a personal rejection. I made it about me rather than about her. Instead of navigating this difference well, it was what I perceived to be the nail in our marriage coffin.

Jill: One of the tools that stops the "Not Accepting" fade is **Acceptance**. These days, I'm valuing Mark's need for touch more than I did in the past. I'm learning that I need it too — just not as much or as often as he desires it. Yet sometimes, I'm sacrificing my need for space in order to meet his need for touch.

I'm also learning how to leverage my strength for good in my marriage. In this, Karen Haught's book *The God-Empowered Wife* was absolutely life-changing for me. I'm reserving my words for when they matter most, resisting commentary on things that just aren't important. I'm also watching the tone I use when I talk to Mark. Karen addresses this in her book when she says:

> We emasculate our husbands by mothering them and then complain they aren't stepping up to the plate. When that doesn't work, we use thinly disguised attempts to control and change them — pushing and prodding them to do what we think they should, or setting a "good example" and hoping they'll get the hint. Eventually, we end up way out front, stretched thin trying to pull our husbands forward and wondering why they aren't cooperating. . . . We become the dominant spouse, even if that wasn't our original intent.[6]

Mark: One night after I had moved out, Jill had been reading Karen Haught's book. When she read the section above, she was very convicted. She called me at nearly 2 a.m. in tears to tell me she was sorry for ever making me feel that way. That phone call was very powerful. It woke me up to the possibility of believing in "us" again.

. . . .

These days I'm speaking up on the now-rare occasion when Jill steps back into "parenting" me. I'm accepting her for who she is and how she's wired. I'm valuing her need for space and not taking that need personally. I'm recognizing that is the way she's made and her need for space is about her and not me. I'm also grateful she is stepping into my world and giving me the gift of touch more often.

Jill: Accepting one another starts with valuing that the way others do things is not wrong—just different. Let's dig into that a bit.

WHY CAN'T YOU JUST BE NORMAL LIKE ME?

When we talk about "differences" in marriage, we're often referring to gender differences. One of the first books on differences that Mark and I read was *His Needs, Her Needs* by Willard Harley. Harley identified ten needs of a marriage but found that when the needs were prioritized, men and women differed. According to Harley, he needs sexual fulfillment, recreational companionship, an attractive spouse, support from home, and admiration. She needs affection, conversation, honesty and openness, financial support, and family commitment.

When Jill and I read the book, we resonated with many of those needs, but they didn't fall quite as neatly into the male/female categories Harley slotted them in. I prioritized some of the needs on the woman's list, and Jill prioritized some of the needs on the man's list. They were valuable differences to understand but didn't seem to get to the bottom of our struggles.

Then we read *The 5 Love Languages* by Gary Chapman. This wonderful resource helped us to better understand how we were each speaking love to each other, but it wasn't in the right language! I (Mark)

. . . .

have the love languages of words of affirmation and physical touch, while Jill's love languages are quality time and acts of service. (You can find out your love languages by taking the free online assessment at www.5lovelanguages.com.)

Once Jill and I started speaking the right language to each other, it brought about positive changes in our relationship!

Even with that information, though, we continued to bump into so many differences. That's when we began to identify some ways we are different that no one seems to talk about. We were tripping over these personality/temperament differences daily because they are so core to how we operate. In fact you could say these traits are our own internal "operating system." They're "cute" when we're dating, but downright frustrating when we deal with them day after day after day. The more we've talked about them with friends, family, and in our speaking and writing, the more we're finding that we're not alone in these frustrations.

What are they? We find that most couples bump into six "operating system" differences. We created a little quiz you can take in the back of the book (it's also available online at www.NoMorePerfectMarriages.com) that will help you determine your own personal "operating system." If your spouse is willing to take the quiz, you can fill in both of your personality traits on page 221. The remainder of this chapter will explain these traits and help you know what to do when your operating systems clash!

Internal Processor/External Processor

An internal processor makes decisions and sorts through facts and feelings in their head. An external processor makes decisions and sorts through facts and feelings in conversation. Both are normal and right ways to process life — they're just different!

Jill is definitely an internal processor. We joke that Jill will think and think about something for days or even weeks and then let me know what "*we*" decided. Although this isn't fully true, it sometimes feels like it! Internal processors need thinking time. Without realizing it, they can gravitate toward isolation. They're often comfortable with quiet and may be the ones who never turn the radio on in the car or the TV on in the house.

Mark is definitely an external processor. Before we understood this, I (Jill) felt like he was wishy-washy in his decision-making. For instance, if we were planning to buy a car, on Tuesday Mark might say, "I think we should go with a Ford. I've been reading about the Ford Taurus . . ." On Wednesday he might continue with, "I'm thinking maybe a Honda Accord would be a good idea . . ." On Thursday, it's yet another automobile brand or model. By this time my internal self is thinking, "My goodness, you're all over the place! Make a decision already!"

External processors often operate as the sports announcers of life.

Internal processors think through the same things inside their head, and they don't usually say something aloud until they're done with their research and have finished the comparing and contrasting inside their head. External processors do all the comparing and contrasting aloud before they make their decision. Once I understood this, I realized Mark wasn't wishy-washy at all. He was simply processing the decision the way God wired him to process: externally!

Another way this can cause challenges in marriage is that external

. . . .

processors often operate as the sports announcers of life. They may comment on every sign as they drive down the road. They speak most of the thoughts that enter their mind. This is normal for them! It's how they are wired to interact with their world. However, it's not normal for an internal processor who thinks many of the same thoughts but keeps them to themselves. The external-processing spouse may long for more communication from the internal-processing mate. The internal-processing spouse may long for a little peace and quiet from all the nonstop narrating.

Mark and I have found that once we understood each other's unique ways of processing, our opposite operating systems actually help each other out. As an internal processor, I (Jill) have found that there are some benefits to sharing my thoughts and feelings when making a decision. I'll never talk things out as much as Mark does, but I'm learning to let him know I'm thinking about something before I'm done thinking about it. He often presents a perspective I hadn't considered or an option I need to add into my thinking. I also have come to understand that his verbal commentary throughout life increases our communication. It keeps us talking, and that deepens intimacy.

I (Mark) have found that Jill's internal processing has helped me to think through things a little more before I speak. I know Jill likes to operate off of facts, figures, and details, so I've learned to gather some of those before I start verbally processing. This is not only helpful for her, but I've found it's helpful for me in making wise decisions.

So how do an internal processor and an external processor live life together? By using their God-tools!

Wisdom will help you gain knowledge about how both you and your spouse are each wired. Wisdom allows you to be in "discovery mode" in your marriage. The more you know and understand yourself, the more you'll then need **courage** to stretch in ways that benefit your marriage. For instance, because I (Jill) am an internal processor, I often find that my family doesn't know when I'm thinking about something. I've had to clue them in when something is on my radar screen. If you're an internal processor, your spouse, children, and even friends may not *really* know you, because you tend to keep your thoughts and emotions inside of you, so you may need courage to open up a little more. An internal processor may need to learn to resist internalizing his or her feelings—because only they know what's happening on the inside. Like me, if you're an internal processor, you may need to learn the value of collaborating and getting other perspectives as you make decisions or solve problems.

External processors will likely need **wisdom** to learn to not fill silent moments in marriage conversations. Because they process aloud, they may view silence as a problem that needs to be fixed. However, if an external processor will learn to ask questions and WAIT, they may very well find out what's going on in their internal-processing spouse's head. This wise step may help external-processing spouses learn not to monopolize conversations. Our external-processing daughter, Erica, says that she finds herself easily overwhelmed if she isn't able to process with someone. This is a place she feels she's growing to better understand herself and how her temperament affects her emotions.

If you'll discover more about who you are and who your spouse is, you'll take your relationship to a deeper place. The more you understand, the less you'll criticize. That alone can change your marriage.

. . . .

Introvert/Extrovert

I (Mark) get to Friday night and think, "It's the weekend, who can we get together with?" Jill gets to Friday and thinks, "I'm so glad it's the weekend because I don't have to see any people until Sunday at church!" Oh my, we are so different!

I used to think that *introvert* and *extrovert* referred to someone's social skills. What I've learned, however, is these two words describe how a person is emotionally refueled. Extroverts are refueled by being with people. Introverts are refueled by being alone.

Jill is an introvert, and she loves being alone. I'm an extrovert and I love being with people. As an introvert, Jill prefers one-on-one conversations. As an extrovert, I enjoy a group setting and love a party. When it comes to friendships—the more the merrier for me! Jill, however, prefers to have just two or three close friends. I confess that I always viewed that as a "defect" in Jill and I criticized that she didn't have more friends. Once I learned that having a small group of friends is characteristic of an introvert, I had to apologize for unfairly judging her.

When navigating this difference in marriage, **compassion** is needed to help you meet in the middle. If you're the extrovert, you need to have compassion and understanding for your spouse's need for quiet. This is how he or she emotionally refuels. If you're the introvert, you'll need to have compassion and understanding for your spouse's need for socializing. This is one way that marriage stretches us and even balances us. Mark's need for socializing keeps me from the temptation many introverts face to isolate. We participate in a small group at church because he likes that kind of interaction with other believers. I also want interaction with other believers, but prefer it in one-on-one

. . . .

settings. However, being a part of a small group is still good for me and it is something Mark and I can do together, since so many of our friends are "my friends" or "Mark's friends" rather than couples.

In the same way, my introvert preference has helped Mark learn to value quiet. He's come to understand that when you pull away from the crowds, you can think deeply. He's also grown to enjoy the value of deep as well as wide relationships.

By the way, being an introvert doesn't automatically make you an internal processor. The same goes for extroverts and external processing. Sometimes you'll find those lining up, but sometimes not. Our daughter is a strong introvert and a strong external processor! So don't make the mistake of assuming if you're one, you'll automatically be the other.

So how do we handle our differing perspectives on weekends? Well, we meet in the middle. We do more socially than I'd prefer, and we do less socially than Mark would prefer. Sometimes Mark gets up and meets a friend for breakfast on Saturday morning, which is something I would probably never do because I love my quiet Saturday mornings! We're true to ourselves while adjusting to each other's needs along the way. We need each other, but we need to understand each other more than anything else!

Medium-High Capacity/Medium-Low Capacity

"Capacity" refers to the emotional capacity we have. It also refers to how many balls you can juggle before it's too much and stress sets in. I (Jill) am medium-high capacity and Mark is medium-low capacity. Both are normal. One is not more "right" than the other. We just have to know ourselves and know our spouse in order to respect and honor both who we are and who they are.

I (Mark) have always told Jill she's not a Type A personality . . . she's Type AAA! The girl keeps going and going and going! When she wakes up in the morning, she is instantly "with it." She can stay up late and still get up early in the morning. That. Is. Not. Me.

This has caused conflict in several ways. Jill has been frustrated because I wasn't keeping up, and I have been frustrated because I always wear out before she does. I've also been frustrated with Jill because she doesn't stop.

Once Jill and I identified the concept of "capacity" and how we were wired with differing capacities, it was a huge revelation for our relationship. Understanding this was both empowering and freeing. We were able to start letting each other off the hook and be our very different selves.

As we learned to live life together, God used our differing capacities to stretch and mold us to be more grace-giving, forgiving, and compassionate with each other. I (Jill) had to learn that even though I could handle doing a lot, it wasn't necessarily healthy for me (spiritually, emotionally, and physically), and it also wasn't healthy for my marriage. Not only that, but my high-capacity choices forced Mark into a high-capacity role too often. For instance, if I said yes to singing on the worship team at church, that required Mark to get the kids ready for church on his own. If I overcommitted, it often committed him in some way as he picked up the childcare or meal or laundry responsibilities I couldn't get to. My high-capacity-do-a-lot choices affected him more than I realized. Even today as we are now mostly empty nesters and we travel together more for speaking, I have to intentionally allow for more margin in our travel plans than when I travel alone. If I'm alone, I can speak in the morning and get on a plane and fly home that evening. Mark just doesn't have that kind of stamina. He wants to have some downtime in the evening and then fly home the next day. This is actually good for both of us, I've come to understand.

In the same way that my (Mark's) medium-low capacity has been good for Jill, her medium-high capacity has been good for me. She helps me persevere when I really want to quit. She keeps me going a little longer when I would have stopped on my own an hour earlier. She helps me to get things done when I feel overwhelmed by the task. God knew what He was doing when He put us together because we balance each other out in so many ways. What I saw as a liability, God designed as an opportunity. I wish I could have seen and valued that earlier in our marriage.

Just like the other differences, when we're dealing with capacity, we have to adjust our expectations of each other. It's human nature to expect others to be "normal" like we are. The more understanding and accepting we are, the less frustrated we get with one another.

Innie/Outie

Nope, we're not talking belly buttons here. This refers to the way we organize our "stuff." Innies tend to file, while outies tend to pile. This outie woman married an innie man and fireworks have happened over the years because of this difference. There's no right or wrong here . . . just different. If we don't understand each other, however, we can find ourselves quickly coming to wrong conclusions about each other.

Innies appear to be very organized because most of their stuff is "in" something. Their mantra is "a place for everything and everything in its place." They like order and dislike clutter.

Outies often have to deal with a little more visual clutter. That's because their mantra might be "Out of sight, out of mind!" Outies might love sticky notes and use them everywhere. (I [Jill] even have digital sticky notes on my computer desktop!) We tend to be pilers rather than filers, because if we file something we might forget about it. Although things may appear cluttered, outies often know exactly what pile something is in!

Jill and I have become a little more like each other without losing ourselves.

Again, our differences have been good for each of us. I (Jill) am an outie who is actually bothered by the clutter caused by my outiness. Mark has taught me some innie organizing principles to tackle the frustration I experienced with my piles. My organizational strategies, however, are still true to my "outie" design. For instance, I have an old picnic basket with a hinged lid on my kitchen counter. Inside the basket are files for my mail and important paperwork that I need to follow up on like invitations, bills, etc. It's on my counter and at my fingertips, but tucked in something so the visual clutter is managed.

For me (Mark), Jill has helped me relax a bit about "stuff." I've learned to find a balance between what I desire and real life. She's helped me have realistic expectations. Jill and I have become a little more like each other without losing ourselves. By using **wisdom** (understanding each other), **grace** (giving each other the freedom to be human), and **forgiveness** (letting each other off the hook when our differences clash), we've allowed God to perfect us to be more like Him in the way we treat each other.

....

Structured/Spontaneous

This part of our temperament has to do with how much planning we prefer. A structured person likes to plan and work the plan. A spontaneous person likes to go with the flow. Structured folks like to have their ducks in a row while spontaneous folks are the free spirits of this world. Both are normal and okay. The problems happen when we bump into each other's preferences.

I (Mark) am the spontaneous one and Jill is more structured. I do value planning and some structure so I'm not extremely spontaneous, but I like to decide what I'm doing based upon how I'm feeling. Jill, on the other hand, has a plan and will usually work that plan no matter how she's feeling. Another way this plays out is I like to come up with an idea and go with it. Jill prefers to let an idea simmer as she internally processes all the pros and cons of this new possibility!

An interesting facet of structured vs. spontaneous is how we each approach surprises. I (Jill) do not like surprises. Mark, on the other hand, loves surprises! Of course, we didn't know this until the first time he threw me a surprise birthday party. I didn't even know that I didn't like surprises until then! I was grateful for all the work he put into making the party happen, but when we talked about it later, I was able to identify that I would probably have enjoyed it more if it hadn't been a surprise. As a structured planner, I spent most of the party trying to adjust my head to the fact that we weren't going out to dinner and a movie, which I truly had my heart set on. My concrete structured mind style couldn't handle the gift of my spontaneous abstract random husband.

Because Mark is more spontaneous and loves surprises, I've learned to put my structured planning self to work to bring surprises to his life.

. . . .

On our anniversary one year I surprised Mark with a hotel key in his anniversary card. I had secretly arranged for the sitter to spend the night, had rented a hotel room earlier in the day, and had already packed us bags that I had taken to the hotel room ahead of time. I gave Mark the card on our "dinner date," and we didn't go home that night. He loved it! I loved planning it. However, if he had planned something like that, I would have hated it. You can call me a killjoy if you want, or you can value differences and recognize we're all fearfully and wonderfully made by a God who knew that this world needed both structured and spontaneous people to get things done!

Jill and I have found that there are some ways I can surprise her. For instance, I can say, "I'm taking you away next weekend." She doesn't have to know where (although she would probably like to!); it just helps her to know that I'm planning something. I guess you could say that it's the same principle as giving your kids a five-minute warning before you want them to pick up toys before bedtime. You're honoring and respecting that they're having fun and may need some transition time to move from what they're enjoying to what they need to do. When I let Jill know I'm planning something, I'm honoring and respecting the planner in her so she can be mentally free to enjoy the time fully.

Again, we've learned to balance each other out. I (Mark) am much more sensitive to the structured people around me, because Jill has helped me value their need for information. I (Jill) am much more inclined to suggest something spontaneous to Mark, because I know he loves that. So on a Saturday that we've worked hard on the house and the yard, I might say midafternoon, "Let's hop on the motorcycle and go out to dinner tonight." Mark loves that kind of spontaneity. He can do the same with me, but he's learned it's helpful to give me a little notice to adjust my planning mind, which probably already had meat thawed for dinner. With a little notice I can tell myself that we can use the meat for Sunday's lunch, and then I can be spontaneous right along with him!

I (Jill) have also had to figure out what is truly a structure preference and what is really my desire to control. Yep, I know that admitting that might be stepping on some toes if you're structured like I am. For instance, if Mark says, "I'm taking you away next weekend," I DO want to know where and what we're doing, but I've learned that is often my desire to control and even pride coming out. He can make those decisions without my input. One way I've learned to discern between the two is to ask myself, "Do I need to know to honor the structured planner in me, or do I want to know because I think I can make a better decision?" Oooooh . . . that's not a fun question to sort through, but it's an important one for sure.

Thinker/Feeler

Usually in marriage, one spouse leans more toward thinking and one leans more toward feeling. In our marriage, as we've already shared, Jill is the thinker and I am the feeler. Thinkers use facts and research to make decisions and interpret their world, while feelers use emotion and intuition.

We first noticed this difference when we were househunting. Jill had a spreadsheet (both on paper and in her head!) with the facts about each house. She kept track of square footage, number of bedrooms and bathrooms, size of yard, miles to the nearest grocery store, distance to school, etc. I, on the other hand, remembered houses by how they felt to me, how the neighborhood felt (did people take care of their yards and take pride in their homes?), and whether I connected with the neighbors while we were there. Honestly, our decisions needed both of these perspectives. Jill tuned in to the tangibles and I tuned in to the intangibles.

A thinker may not notice subtle signals and not sense when their mate has a need.

Where this gets challenging in marriage is that each person needs something from the other that they have to work harder to give. For instance, as a thinker, I (Jill) want Mark to give me facts and research when we need to make a decision. That's secondary to him so he has to work a little harder at it. As a feeler, Mark wants me to connect with him emotionally, and that's not always the easiest thing for me to do. I have to dig a little deeper to really know what I "feel" about something. Also, a thinker may not notice subtle signals and not sense when there is something wrong or their mate has a need. If the feeler mate understands this, he/she can learn to communicate with words to indicate a need. For instance, Mark has learned to say, "I need you to know I'm feeling overwhelmed with this and need a little bit of grace." I'm so appreciative of this communication because I often don't "read" those signals.

For those who are feelers, it's also helpful to know if you fall on the "highly sensitive" spectrum. Highly sensitive people seem to have extra antennae that are sensing the environment around them. Sometimes their sensitivity is physical, dealing with smell, touch, sound, and tasting. Sometimes their sensitivity is more emotional, responding to emotional overload or overstimulation. I (Mark) fall into the highly sensitive spectrum. Understanding this has been really helpful for both Jill and me and probably links up with my low-capacity temperament too. I can become easily overwhelmed if I don't manage my to-do list well.

I also didn't always handle the chaos of five kids well. I wish I'd understood why twenty years ago — because then Jill and I could have made some important adjustments in our expectations and how we handled high-stress, chaotic situations. Usually that was when my anger would kick in and I would use rage to "gain control." Now I know that was a false control, but it was all I knew at the time. Understanding our emotional wiring is so important for handling life well. (You can learn more about high sensitivity at www.hsperson.com.)

Of course one of the best ways to work as a thinker/feeler team is to operate within our strengths. When we're planning a trip or making a purchase, Mark will often ask me to do the research. I'm usually happy to do that. If Mark senses something is wrong with one of our kids, I've learned to trust him. His discernment meter is far more sensitive than mine and I don't always notice subtleties in their demeanor. Usually he's right! When we learn to trust each other's strengths, we're less likely to be frustrated by them. This is when we're better together!

DIFFERENCES AREN'T DEFICIENCIES

Differences aren't labels. They're not excuses. They're most certainly not deficiencies. Differences are the personality and temperament traits that describe how we process the world around us. We start by understanding ourselves first and then we move to understand our spouse better. (If you have kids, this might also give you some insight into better understanding your kids, too!)

Marriage (and parenting) challenges happen when we think the way we do things is the right way or the only way. The fade starts with criticizing, moves to "trying to change," and if not stopped ends up at rejection. When we begin to understand and accept our spouses for who they are, we are making important progress!

The more we understand, the more we use **wisdom, acceptance, and compassion.** This allows our spouse to be who God created him or her to be. Let's stop the fade of "not accepting" and commit today to look at differences through a different lens. We promise you'll turn your frustration into fascination!

❖ THINK ABOUT IT ❖

Where do you need to be more accepting of your spouse? Where have you been trying to control or force change? Is there any place you've been rejecting? Are differences the start of a slow fade in your marriage? If so, you can begin to turn around today!

❖ TALK ABOUT IT ❖

My biggest takeaway from this chapter was_____

_____

_____

This is how I feel about surprises:_____

_____

_____

Here is how we're each wired:

	Husband	Wife
Love Language		
Internal/External Processor		
Introvert/Extrovert		
Medium High/Medium Low Capacity		
Innie/Outie		
Structured/Spontaneous		
Thinker/Feeler		

⚜ TALK TO GOD ABOUT IT ⚜

Lord, You're creative for sure. You've made each one of us with unique strengths, personalities, sensitivities, and temperaments. Help me to better understand myself and to better understand _____. Convict me when I jump to judgment or am tempted to criticize. If criticism exits my mouth, give me the courage to apologize and ask for forgiveness. Help me to watch the tone of my communication and to pay attention to the nonverbal communication I use. Help me to celebrate _____'s uniqueness and be grateful for how he/she is different from me. In Jesus' Name. Amen.

Today's Truth: "Accept one another, then, just as Christ accepted you, in order to bring praise to God." ROMANS 15:7

THE DISHES GO IN THE DISHWASHER ONLY *One Way*

THE SLOW FADE OF DISAGREEMENT

We live in an old farmhouse built in 1912. While it has wonderful space, a fabulous location, and endearing history, nothing is square in this old house. This has become even more evident as we have renovated our kitchen over the past ten months.

Mark and I have rarely given too much thought to our decorating styles. Because we've always lived on a pretty tight budget, our shared style has been "Late American Scavenger" for much of our married life. Even in our kitchen remodel, we built our new kitchen island out of a cabinet found on the curb. One family's trash became our family's treasure!

· · · · · · · ·

After we installed our new ceramic tile backsplash, that's where we discovered lines. Or the fact that I don't like lines unless they're straight. Remember the fact that nothing is square in our home? Yep, lines and not square are a problem. So we may be redecorating our redecorating sooner rather than later.

Does any of this bother Mark? Nope. Not at all. Some of the electrical boxes were put in crooked, so the electrical switch plates sit a little crooked on the wall. Mark is unwilling to tear out a whole wall in our home in order to straighten an electrical box. I, on the other hand, would be happy to live with the dust and disorder for a few more months to get those boxes straight. Can you say disagreement?

We've already established that husbands and wives are very different people. They each have their own personalities, temperaments, and experiences that will likely differ from each other in some way. This alone can be the source of much conflict and disagreement. When you add in each of our own fears, opinions, preferences, and beliefs, you've just increased the frequency of disagreement. Left untouched, disagreement will pull you apart when you need to be coming together.

So what do we do? How can we disagree and move toward each other instead of away from each other? Here's our story:

Mark: One of the best things Jill and I have done is to dig in to our personality styles to understand how God made us. But even more importantly has been for us to dig in to EACH OTHER'S personality style to understand how God made this person we live with every day. Too many of our disagreements have started there. Even if we better understand each other, we can still have differing perspectives that cause disagreement.

. . . .

Jill: I'm not particularly fond of conflict, but I do know it's part of merging two lives together. Figuring out how to "meet in the middle" has been a learning curve for me, though, because I tend to base my position on facts that make sense in my black-and-white brain. Because arguments engage my analytical brain, I can argue my point a little too well at times.

Mark: Since Jill has already stated that she doesn't like conflict, I will admit right up front that I don't like conflict, either. Figuring out how to "meet in the middle" and not take the "loss" of that middle ground personally has been a learning curve for me. Because I'm a feeler, I also feel the emotions of conflict very strongly. When disagreement takes so much emotional energy out of me, I can go passive a little too easily.

Over the years I've learned the importance of giving up the "right to be right" for the sake of relationship.

Jill: Growing up, I didn't experience a lot of conflict. This, however, didn't mean that we always agreed. It just meant that we didn't engage our disagreements—if we disagreed with someone, we would let it go rather than responding. Initially I didn't know how to engage disagreement. In time, however, I learned to use my fact-finding skills to load my conflict gun. It wasn't healthy, but it was effective for winning arguments. Over the years I've learned the importance of giving up the "right to be right" for the sake of relationship.

Mark: Growing up, disagreement was anything but healthy. My biological father was a passive man who would stuff his feelings until he became angry and enraged. My stepfather allowed no one to have an opinion or thought of their own. You could only have his. He managed conflict with rage and violence. I came into marriage a nice, passive guy who had no opinions (that were voiced, anyway) and would stuff my thoughts until I burst open and raged. It wasn't until later in married life that I took this seriously, sought counseling, and determined to handle conflict in a healthier way.

Jill: Disagreeing is actually an important part of marriage. You will disagree. You need to disagree. However, it's the fade that happens AFTER disagreement that we need to pay attention to. Mark and I both had different, but equally unhealthy, fades after disagreement.

Mark: I experienced two fades with disagreement. I would either *Disagree → Argue → Control (Rage)* or I would *Become Passive → Withdraw →, Deceive.* (Do what I want behind the scenes.) Neither of these was healthy, but they are the reality many of us start to ride out in marriage if we don't do something to stop it. Too often my shame further fueled my wrong direction. I would argue and/or rage in order to control the situation. However, even raging would fuel my shame, so I'd eventually withdraw and over time choose deception, functioning one way on the outside and another way on the inside. Many times, I would also yield to passivity, believing the fight wasn't worth it. This fed my feelings of hopelessness.

Jill: My direction after differing opinions was different than Mark's. Mine was *Disagree → Control → Crush.* Too often my pride would fuel me as I worked harder to win than to listen. I pushed and prodded to control and in doing so, would too often crush my husband's spirit. When winning is more important than listening, or when a spouse feels their way is the right way and their spouse's way is the wrong way, it is crushing to their partner who doesn't feel heard or valued.

Mark: One antidote to my disagreement fade is speaking up with

courage. These days if we disagree (and we still do plenty often!), I'm working to sort out what she's saying from how she's saying it. She can have the tiniest bit of authority in her voice and I used to get snagged by that. Today I'm recognizing that is Jill's strength coming through and what she's saying still has value. I'm also letting her know that I've heard her and value her perspective, even if I don't agree with it. That helps her to stop her fade before it starts. She doesn't need to control, because she's been heard and validated.

Jill: Humility has helped me turn things around. I've decided it's more important to *do* what's right than it is to *be* right. These days I'm reserving my thoughts for when they really matter. I'm letting Mark make decisions I used to want to weigh in on. It may seem silly, but one of the biggest places I'm keeping my mouth shut is when he is driving. I'm all about efficiency and getting something done the quickest, most logical way. Mark doesn't care. Both ways get us from point A to point B, so I'm learning to be okay with the scenic route!

Mark: We're also both applying the antidotes of **grace** and **forgiveness**. Grace allows us both to be human and different and unique; forgiveness helps us when we bump into our imperfections.

When disagreement happens, you and your spouse probably head into one of these wrong directions or one of your own. The most important thing to do is to identify what happens inside of you when you and your partner disagree, then turn things around with courage, humility, grace, forgiveness, or whatever God-tool best addresses your heart condition.

We will see things differently than our spouse does. We will have different perspectives. We will have different opinions. Learning what to do with those incongruities can stop the slow fade of disagreement in its tracks. Let's hone our God-honoring conflict resolution skills and explore some common areas of disagreement in marriage along the way.

GET TO THE HEART OF THE MATTER

In marriage it's all about you. All about your attitude, that is. When you experience conflict, the first step is to get to the heart of the matter. If you can, step away and ask yourself a few questions:

Am I making a mountain out of a molehill? When I (Jill) was younger, my dad would often use that phrase. It's stuck with me into my adult years and I've used it as a question to think through both marriage and parenting conflict. Sometimes, I'm making something into a bigger deal than it really needs to be.

What's really going on inside of me? Whatever you're fighting about is secondary to what is *really* going on. The heart of conflict can be anxiety, fear, disappointment, hurt, pride, selfishness, control, stress, feeling overwhelmed, insecurity, expectations, exhaustion, depression, and even imposing past hurts from parents on an unsuspecting spouse. The quicker you can identify what's going on inside of you, the better it is for navigating your part of the disagreement. This is living out Matthew 7:5: "First take the plank out of your own eye, and then you will see clearly to remove the speck from your brother's eye."

What do I need to reframe? If I'm seeing my spouse as my enemy, I need to remember we're really on the same team. If I'm imposing past hurts from my childhood on my spouse, I need to remind myself that "my wife is not my stepfather" or "my husband is not my mom." If I'm pointing the finger at my partner, I need to pay attention to the three fingers pointing back to me and ask myself what I'm contributing negatively to this disagreement. If I'm slipping into "he always . . ." or "she never . . ." thinking, I need to stop myself from globalizing this issue and move back to localizing it to the situation at hand.

Am I addressing this directly, or resorting to a passive-aggressive reaction? Passive-aggressive reactions include sarcasm, trying to guilt your spouse into doing something, manipulation, punishing by withholding sex, withdrawing, silent treatment, and intentional inefficiency (doing something halfway).

There's a reason God gave us two eyes, two ears, and one mouth.

Yes, growth involves pain. Coming face-to-face with our unhealthy responding patterns is painful, but also maturing. This is how we live out Hebrews 12:11: "No discipline seems pleasant at the time, but painful. Later on, however, it produces a harvest of righteousness and peace for those who have been trained by it."

RESPOND, DON'T REACT

There's a reason God gave us two eyes, two ears, and one mouth. Our words are powerful. The Bible addresses this in dozens of verses that remind us to guard our tongue, measure our words, and be careful about the kind of answer we give. Here are just a few of God's words of wisdom for us:

"Whoever keeps his mouth and his tongue keeps himself out of trouble." PROVERBS 21:23 (ESV)

"Do not let any unwholesome talk come out of your mouths, but only what is helpful for building others up according to their needs, that it may benefit those who listen." EPHESIANS 4:29 (NIV)

"A soft answer turns away wrath, but a harsh word stirs up anger." PROVERBS 15:1 (ESV)

"There is one whose rash words are like sword thrusts, but the tongue of the wise brings healing." PROVERBS 12:18 (ESV)

"Set a guard, O LORD, over my mouth; keep watch over the door of my lips!" PSALM 141:3 (ESV)

That's only the beginning. Our words matter—a lot. With our words we can start a fire or put out a fire. We can bring life or death to a relationship. We can go to battle or defuse the conflict with our words. With that in mind, let's look at six disarming phrases you can learn to use more often during conflict:

Tell me more. This phrase lets your loved one know you're listening. It invites him/her to share their whole heart and everything they are thinking on the topic of conversation. Here's an example of how we've used it. Mark had a rough day at work the other day. He expressed his frustration. I sat down at the dinner table with him and said, "You mentioned it was a rough day. Tell me more."

....

What I hear you saying is . . . This phrase reflects back to your partner what you have heard them say. Think of it as the same concept of what happens when you order fast food in the drive-through lane. You place your order and they repeat it back to you. Then you either correct them if they got it wrong or you let them know they have it right. When you're using this with your spouse, it doesn't mean you agree with what he or she is saying; it simply means you've heard what he or she is saying.

I agree with you on . . . When you can find one or more things you agree upon concerning the issue being discussed, it helps remind you both you're on the same team and sets the pace for working together. Once you've established what you both agree on, the issues of disagreement often don't look so large. We recently used this when we were discussing connecting with our son, who has some pretty severe mental health issues. Mark wanted to invite him and his "friends" (many who have been in trouble with the law) over for a cookout. I responded with, "I agree with you that we should work to stay connected. However, I would feel more comfortable meeting on neutral ground."

I . . . *(rather than "you")* Using "I statements" helps to keep defensiveness out of the picture. "You" blames while "I" explains. For example, "I feel disrespected and parented when you speak to me like that," is far more effective than "You always parent me and I'm sick of it."

I receive that. Maybe your spouse has expressed frustration that you have once again been too controlling. You know he or she is right and is holding you accountable. "I receive that" lets your spouse know that they are correct and you've heard what they are saying. Often an apology and asking for forgiveness might follow. Jill just used this statement the other day. I expressed some frustration about how she had handled a situation. She thought about it for a moment and said, "I receive that. I need to think about it a little more, but I receive what you're saying." It was so helpful to know that she accepted my feedback.

I'm sorry. Will you please forgive me? Too often we cut our apologies short with just "I'm sorry." Asking for forgiveness puts a question on the table to the party who was offended or hurt. Once they are able to offer forgiveness, closure is experienced in the conflict and the broken place in the relationship can be restored.

CONFLICT SIGHTINGS

The Bible reminds us that "there is nothing new under the sun" (Eccl. 1:9b). While conflict is deeply personal and almost always stressful, there are common topics most married couples argue over. If we're aware of them, and incorporate some wise proactive strategies, we can more likely reduce conflict.

Parenting

Because we were raised in different families, our parenting styles naturally will differ. Even if we declare that we'll "never parent like I was parented," the truth is we will likely repeat how we were parented unless we actively learn to replace it with something else. The issue with parenting conflict is where you sort it out. One of the most used phrases in our home when we were actively parenting was "step into my office," which meant "meet me in the bathroom to discuss this issue." This was our way of discussing and sometimes disagreeing behind closed doors. It was here that we sorted out our differences. Not in front of the kids. The most important thing to do as parents is to present a united front.

Even now as our kids are older, we still have to navigate parenting differences. Nobody tells you how challenging parenting is after your kids become adults! "Can you help us with the kids?" "Can you help us financially?" "Can we live with you for a while?" "Can you help us fix our house?" We've learned to navigate these questions and others in the past few months.

If you're in a blended family, it is extremely important that you determine how to parent as a team with his kids, her kids, and our kids. A united front is doubly important when merging two families. Work together behind the scenes to create the goals and guidelines that will create the home environment you want for everyone who spends time together in your home.

Proactive Strategy: Learn about parenting together. One of the best things we did was to attend a parenting conference and take several different courses at church together. Why was this important? It got us on the same page. We heard the same teaching and processed the same information. We didn't necessarily agree with everything we learned, but taking the classes together gave us a shared vocabulary and forced conversation that helped us set our own strategies in place. Other ways to learn together include watching a parenting video together, reading a parenting book together (check out the *No More Perfect Kids* book and videos at www.NoMorePerfect.com), or listen to a parenting podcast and discuss what you're learning.

. . . .

Sex

Let's face it. One of you probably wants it more and one of you probably wants it less. It's a common issue in most marriages and it causes quite a bit of conflict. Complicating matters are pregnancy, contraception, breast-feeding, post-pregnancy emotions and physical changes, exhaustion, menopause, erectile dysfunction, pornography, and a history of sexual abuse, just to name a few.

Sex is something most of us aren't particularly comfortable talking about. This keeps us from addressing our differing drives and processing our feelings along the way. For most of our marriage I (Mark) have thought about sex once every seventeen seconds and Jill has thought about it once every seventeen days. Seriously, we've been at opposite ends of the spectrum. Somewhere in her forties, Jill's desire actually increased, and, wouldn't you know it, mine actually decreased. So even when my wildest dreams came true, we were still opposites. Counseling helped us deal with some of the baggage we brought into our marriage, including pornography and premarital sex. It also helped us learn to talk about sex more outside the bedroom.

Proactive Strategy #1: Talk about it (outside the bedroom with clothes on so you feel less vulnerable!). Here are some conversation starters to begin discussing what you need to be talking about:

What do you like best about our sex life?
What do you wish was different in our sex life?
Is there something I do sexually that bothers you?
Is there something I do sexually that you really like?
Ideally, how often would you like us to make love?

Foreplay . . . is it too long, too short, or just right for you?

What happens outside the bedroom in our relationship that hurts our intimacy inside the bedroom?

Do I make you feel special outside the bedroom?

When it comes to communication, what do you wish we talked about more?

Do you feel emotionally safe with me? If not, what could I do to help you feel safe?

Is there anything either one of us needs to talk to a doctor about that would improve our sex life (erectile dysfunction, vaginal dryness, pain during intercourse, depression, unusually low desire, etc.)?

Is there any emotional or sexual baggage from your past or any struggles today that are keeping you from fully enjoying sex (pornography, previous relationships, guilt, shame, etc.)?

Is there something in our marriage relationship that we can't seem to improve or get past? What counselor could we begin seeing to sort through this?

Proactive Strategy #2: Schedule sex. One of the best things Mark and I did for our sex life was to schedule sex. Sound crazy? We thought so too. In time, however, it transformed our sex life. Consider these advantages:

It eliminates "The Ask": In most marriages, one partner possesses a higher desire than the other and requests sex more often, while his or her partner rarely asks for physical intimacy. For the spouse with a higher desire, the fear of rejection often sets in. One becomes weary of having to ask, or even beg, for sex on a regular basis. When a couple can agree upon a basic schedule for sex in marriage, it takes the guesswork out. While this still leaves room for occasional spontaneity, it reassures the higher-sex-drive mate that it will happen, and not only that—they know *when!* Usually the schedule is less often than the partner with a higher desire would want and more frequent than the partner with a lesser desire may want. Instead, it's meeting on middle ground.

It increases desire: For the partner with a diminished desire, scheduling sex engages the brain, the largest sex organ in the human body. The brain needs to be clued to prepare the body for a sexual response. Most people who have a lower sexual drive simply don't think about sex very often. Scheduling jump-starts this process. Once sex is on the calendar, it provides a reminder to think about sex, prepares us mentally for being together physically, and primes us to "get in the mood."

"Jill, you're trying to go from making meatloaf to making love in thirty seconds flat? You can't do that!"

When I (Jill) complained to a friend about having trouble getting in the mood, she said, "Jill, you're trying to go from making meatloaf to making love in thirty seconds flat? You can't do that. You have to have a strategy for going from point A to point B." She was right!

Rarely does the partner with an increased desire need to get "in the mood." In contrast, the partner with a lesser desire may need to work at it. When sex is on the calendar, though, it serves as a prompt to set strategies in motion. Scheduling sex reminds spouses that they're working together toward the goal of intimacy, valuing their appointed rendezvous, and doing whatever it takes to make it happen.

It increases anticipation: When lovemaking is kept on the front burner, it builds anticipation. Both husband and wife begin to prepare for their marital recreation. Have you ever thought of sex as recreation? It is! God gave us the gift of sex as a form of recreation in our marriage. It's our own private playground, where God intends for us to enjoy physical pleasure.

When sex is on the schedule, we enjoy planning our time together, because we both hold the same goal. We can even become lifelong learners of giving pleasure to each other. Keeping a couple of Christian sexual technique books on the shelf may develop us into connoisseurs of giving physical pleasure to each other, and it builds anticipation as we think about the next time we'll be together.

It allows for prime-time planning: He prefers nighttime when he can be romantic. She prefers daytime when she's not so tired. They decide that twice-a-week lovemaking is on their calendar—Tuesday at noon (he comes home for lunch and she arranges a sitter for the kids) and Friday at night (after a warm bath and an evening of watching a movie together or going out on a date). This schedule worked well for one couple we mentored.

Most couples not only differ in their desires concerning frequency of sex, but also in the atmosphere that's conducive to sex. Some struggle with making love anytime children are in the vicinity. Others prefer a certain time of the day. When you put your lovemaking on the calendar, you can work to accommodate those likes/dislikes to meet the needs of both.

It helps couples prepare physically: I (Jill) used to tease Mark that once we got on a lovemaking schedule, it sure took the pressure off shaving my legs every day! On a serious side, there's value in preparing yourself physically to make love to your mate. A hot bath or shower, a freshly shaved body, and some great-smelling lotion often relax us for physical intimacy. It also builds anticipation as you prepare to be with your spouse. If weariness keeps you from being excited about sex, an early evening nap may be just the key if lovemaking is on the agenda that night. Since some of the guesswork is out of the mix, we can prepare not only mentally but physically.

It builds trust: If we're going to commit to lovemaking on a regular basis, we need to honor our word and agreement. When we honor our word, it builds trust and deepens intimacy. On the rare occasion that something prevents your regularly scheduled lovemaking, spouses need to communicate their value of sexual intimacy so they can make alternate plans to meet those physical and emotional needs. This is the key to successfully calendaring your intimacy.

We've learned that spontaneous sex may have its place in life, but scheduling sex always has its place on our calendar!

Money

One of you is probably a spender and one of you is probably a saver. They say opposites attract and indeed they do in all areas of life — money included! Money conflict, however, isn't always about dollars and cents. It's often more about generosity, freedom, security, power, lifestyle, and general beliefs about spending and saving.

Too often we only talk about money when we disagree. Instead we should be having "budget committee meetings" on a regular basis to determine money management strategies together. It's likely one of you will be the "bookkeeper" and be responsible for paying the bills, but both need to be involved in budget decisions. Here are some conversation starters for talking about money:

. . . .

How do you feel about money?

What does not having money mean to you?

How was money managed in the home you grew up in?

What do you feel about tithing and giving generously?

Do you feel secure about our financial future?

What financial fears do you have?

Proactive Strategy: Take a money management class together. Just like parenting, one of the best things Mark and I did was to sign up for Dave Ramsey's Financial Peace University course at a local church. This gave us a shared vocabulary and opened up the opportunity for money conversations. It also helped us start our budget committee meetings. (Find a Financial Peace class in your area at www.daveramsey.com/fpu.)

Division of Duties

This is often a place where unknown, unspoken, and unmet expectations just might exist. Many of those expectations may come from how each of your parents handled the division of duties when you were growing up. If you grew up in a home where the wife stayed home and handled the cooking, cleaning, and kids, while the husband handled the yard, home repair, and bringing home the bacon, you may have come into marriage expecting the same division of duties. However, if your spouse grew up with both parents working and both chipping in at home, your clashing expectations may cause fireworks.

It's best to have conversations about how to handle household chores in a neutral setting—not when you're in the thick of conflict.

. . . .

Sometime when you're driving somewhere or you're out on a date, ask each other these questions:

When you think about cooking, cleaning, laundry, yardwork, grocery shopping, decorating, helping with homework, bathing the kids, and bedtime routine, what is "no big deal" for you to do?

When you think about those same things, what stresses you out the most?

Can we divide duties based upon what least stresses us and is easiest for us to do?

Is there anything both of us don't like to do? How could we handle that well together?

Is there anything we can "outsource"? (To the kids? To hire out?)

Proactive Strategy: Play to your strengths. Most conflict happens when one of us is keeping score. Trying to make things "fair" never works because life circumstances change availability all the time. Instead look at each other's strengths and determine the division of duties that way. For instance, I can manage our money quickly and with less stress than Mark can. He, on the other hand, handles home repairs like a champ. With both of us working now, we often make dinner together as we share about our day. Find what works for you, throw a servant heart into the mix to help each other out, and you'll reduce conflict in this area of life!

In-laws

You each came from a family you will likely need to maintain relationship with. Some in-laws bring joy to your marriage; and, as some of us know, some in-laws bring pain to your marriage. The struggle is real.

There's a reason the Bible tells us we are to "leave and cleave." The wording of the English Standard Version of Genesis 2:24 says it this way: "Therefore a man shall leave his father and his mother and hold fast to his wife, and they shall become one flesh." This verse spells out what it looks like to shift your relationship priorities. Until you're married, your parents may be the most important people in your life. Once you marry, your spouse becomes the most important person in your life. Therefore your spouse is your first consideration. He or she is to be protected and prioritized.

Sometimes conflict happens when one spouse throws the other spouse under the bus in conversations with extended family. We need to know that we're always respected and protected when we're with each other's families. Early in our marriage, Mark would use "humor" in extended family settings to send digs my way. I felt "sold out" for the sake of a laugh. When I talked with him about it, he didn't even realize he was doing it and promised to change. He did, and once again my feelings of being respected and protected were restored.

Often with extended family relationships, you have to step up and set boundaries with your own family. If your parents keep showing up unannounced and that really bothers your spouse, you'll need to ask your parents to call before coming over. If your extended family is disrespectful to your spouse, you'll have to be the one to address that and require respect. If they can't seem to turn it around, you may have to decide to reduce the amount of time you spend with certain family members. That may be disappointing to you and to them, but it speaks volumes to your spouse that he/she is more important. What do you

What do you owe your in-laws? You owe them kindness, respect, and consistent Christian character and behavior.

owe your in-laws? You owe them kindness, respect, and consistent Christian character and behavior.

Proactive Strategy: Talk about it. Ask your spouse, "Is there any way you don't feel protected or prioritized in our marriage when it comes to my family?" Then pay attention to what answer you get and determine to make some changes. You may be tempted to disagree or even blame your spouse for the family dynamics, but resist the urge to do that. Remember, you're on one team working together to strengthen your marriage relationship, stop any fades caused by disagreement, and move closer together.

Hobbies/Vacations/Free Time

Vacations are one thing Jill and I actually agree upon! We both like to go somewhere relaxing and do absolutely nothing. Whew! Finally an area where we're not opposites. However, we know that's not the experience many couples have. One wants to go, go, go, and the other wants to just chill. One family we know ran into vacation disagreement because he grew up going to his family's cabin on the lake every summer. Her family, however, went to various vacation spots over the years. When they got married, he assumed vacation meant the lake, and she thought vacation meant a unique destination each year! When these kinds of challenges show up, this is where you have to meet in the middle in some way.

Proactive Strategy: Step into each other's world. When I (Mark) started riding a motorcycle, Jill was initially very fearful of riding with me. In the beginning she said that she'd rather that be "my thing" and not an "us thing." I'm so glad she pushed through her fears and eventually decided to join me, because it's become something we can do together. (I [Jill] am also glad I did. I'm much more relaxed these days when we ride!)

When Jill steps into my world like that, it makes me much more inclined to step into her world. She loves going to plays and musicals. They're not my favorite thing to do, but I'm willing to make that happen on occasion because I know it brings her joy.

Couple Time

While most couples agree on the need to spend time together, many find themselves in conflict, navigating the logistics of making it happen. Sometimes the conflict is over leaving the children or finding childcare. Other times the conflict is more about the finances of making couple time happen. Still other couples find themselves in conflict over what activities they do when it's just the two of them.

Mark and I have found that there are three types of dates we need to be having: daily dates, weekly (biweekly or monthly) dates, and annual getaways. Is it easy to make these happen? Not usually. Is it important? Absolutely.

Daily dates are just the daily connections we have as a couple. A phone call over lunch. A text that says, "I'm thinking of you." A note in your lunch box. These small acts of kindness keep you moving together rather than apart.

Weekly dates are regular times you set aside to spend time together. Weekly is ideal, but biweekly or monthly dates are better than nothing! These kinds of regular dates are planned in advance, on the calendar,

....

and protected. Maybe they happen every Friday, or every other Tuesday, or the fourth Saturday of every month. If you have kids at home, you arrange for a college student to babysit, or grandma and grandpa to take care of the kids, or you trade sitting with another couple who also want to take regular date nights. These important times of uninterrupted conversation and focus on each other keep you investing in your relationship when everyday life responsibilities threaten to pull you apart.

Then there are the annual getaways. Taking some time for a twenty-four-hour to one-week getaway for just the two of you allows you to remember what it's like to play and explore the world together. It gets you away from the daily routines that keep you in relational ruts. If you save fifteen dollars a month from one anniversary to the next anniversary, you'll have enough saved for a twenty-four-hour getaway every year!

Special note to those of you with little ones: resist the urge to think, *We'll take time for us after the kids are gone.* Push through your fear of leaving the kids. You did not take a marriage vow that you would "love, honor, and cherish you until kids do us part." You are a wife first and a mother second. You are a husband first and a father second. Your kids need to see you prioritize your marriage. They'll find security in knowing that mommy and daddy are okay. Make spending time as a couple your priority today!

Proactive Strategy: Talk about it. Take each of the types of dates mentioned above and brainstorm ways to make these happen. Put dates on the calendar, set up a savings account for an annual getaway budget, set goals for things to do and places to see together. Move forward with a "we" mindset that keeps you having fun together!

. . . .

GET OUT YOUR TOOLBOX

Disagreement often brings out the worst in us. Our efforts to be heard, to force our spouse to agree with us, and to get our way, put "me" before "we." When we navigate disagreement, we need **courage** to broach topics we may not be comfortable talking about. **Grace** allows us to be human, different, and unique. **Forgiveness** is what we use when we step on each other's toes and bump into each other's imperfections in disagreement. **Humility** is needed when our pride wants to win rather than listen. It helps us remember to *do* what is right rather than *be* right. **Compassion** is desperately needed when "walking in my spouse's shoes" can help me better hear and understand his or her perspective. **Acceptance** allows us to differ and disagree, keeping us from trying to change each other. **Wisdom** tells us that when conflict becomes (or seems) too big to get to the other side of it, we need to seek help from a mentor or a counselor.

Finally, **love** is patient and kind. It keeps us from being arrogant or rude. It is not irritable or resentful. It "bears all things, believes all things, hopes all things, endures all things" (1 Corinthians 13:4–7 ESV).

❧ THINK ABOUT IT ❧

What can you do today to change how you will respond the next time you and your spouse disagree? Of the common conflicts couples have, which one could you be more proactive about to minimize conflict?

❧ TALK ABOUT IT ❧

My biggest takeaway from this chapter was_____
_____

I've never given it much thought, but I can see that my slow fade dynamic with disagreement is_____
_____

When dealing with disagreement, I realize that I most need to use my God-tools of _____
_____

Brainstorm together a fun date you can plan and get on the calendar!

❧ TALK TO GOD ABOUT IT ❧

God, there are so many places where it's easy to disagree. I want my way and _____ wants his/her way. Help me to move from a "me" to a "we" mindset. Show me how to listen, how to receive feedback, how to speak kindly, and how to give generously in my marriage. Help me to give disarming responses when things get tense between the two of us.

More than anything, help me to keep my heart softened to Your ways. Less of me and more of You, Lord. In Jesus' Name. Amen.

Today's Truth: "Do not let any unwholesome talk come out of your mouths, but only what is helpful for building others up according to their needs, that it may benefit those who listen." EPHESIANS 4:29

## CHAPTER 8

"I'M NOT *Overreacting!*"

THE SLOW FADE OF DEFENSIVENESS

*T*hey sat in our living room sorting through the emotions of their hurting relationship. This couple, married more than twenty years, had asked Mark and me for help navigating some challenges they couldn't seem to work through on their own. With great courage, the husband gingerly communicated how his wife had made him feel just a few days before. He used "I" statements and worked hard to communicate clearly and kindly.

But she squashed him. Exasperated, she defended her actions from earlier in the week. Her logic was sensible. She had good, rational reasons for how she had handled the situation. However, she wasn't hearing her husband at all. Her logic undermined her love. Reasons should never trump relationship. Yet when we're defensive, that's exactly what happens.

Here's our story:

Mark: While we had drastically improved our communication and conflict resolution through years of marriage counseling, we still had unhealthy undercurrents beneath the surface of our relationship. When our conflicts went unresolved because either or both of us were responding defensively, I would isolate internally.

Jill: I would do the same thing. The slow fade of defensiveness moves from unresolved conflict to isolation. I would "lick my wounds" privately and internally rationalize why I was right. Too often I didn't seek to understand.

Mark: My isolation eventually led to disengagement. Externally I behaved as if everything were okay, but internally I was putting up fences and harboring hurt. I was like the child who says yes on the outside and no on the inside. Many times the root of this comes from our childhood. If we grow up in an emotionally unsafe home, we learn early to agree on the outside to keep the peace. Internally, we tuck the hurt in to our heart, building a case of bitterness. It's not healthy, but it's a form of protection some of us may have used to survive in our formative years.

During our healing process, I worked to match my outside to my insides with courageous, humble conversation. In time, my tendency to defend decreased.

Jill: In order to stop the slow fade of defensiveness, we have to start in those early moments of frustration. What we do in those initial minutes of disagreement will often set the direction for our communication. Dialing down our anger and dialing into God's perspective makes a huge difference.

Mark: When we defend, we don't listen. We don't own our own stuff. We don't consider how we might not be right or fully right. **Humility**, on the other hand, requires us to listen. It requires us to evaluate ourselves and own our stuff. Humility approaches conflict with a heart that says, "What is my part in this?"

Jill: Humility and pride can't exist in the same room. You have to get rid of pride to find humility. As the familiar Bible verse says, "Pride goes before destruction, a haughty spirit before a fall" (Proverbs 16:18). It also tells us that we have to push past *what we want to do* and replace it with *what we need to do*.

Mark: Marriage is really about growing us up, maturing us emotionally and spiritually. It's about learning to die to self in a healthy way because we're becoming more like Christ. Jesus Christ didn't WANT to go to the cross, but He knew that He NEEDED to. I don't WANT to look at myself when Jill and I are navigating conflict, but I know that I NEED to. This helps me not to be defensive.

Jill: I don't WANT to lay down my pride because it's a form of self-preservation. But God's Word tells me He is my Defender—I don't need to step into that role—it's already filled!

Mark: Don't worry if your spouse isn't working toward being less defensive. Stopping the painful cycles in a marriage can start with one person. You *can* make a difference by dialing down your defensiveness and simply engaging your spouse differently than you have in the past. If we dismantle the habit of defensiveness, we can engage more compassionately and openly in our relationship. Let's look at why we're defensive and some practical steps to make change happen.

....

DIALOGUE OR DEBATE?

I (Jill) once heard someone say that to be defensive is to react with a war mentality to a nonwar issue. Defensiveness is an overreaction that causes us to arm ourselves with emotional weapons. Left untended, defensiveness contributes to what author Sheldon Vanauken calls a "creeping separateness."

Defensiveness causes us to revert to our respective corners. You stop sharing information or talking about things that matter because you don't want to start World War III in your living room. As a form of protection or even just habit, you focus more on "I" and "me" than "we." Before you know it, you've created the great divide right in the middle of your relationship and you don't know how to close the gap.

We all end up in a defensive position at some time or another. The question isn't if it will happen, it's how quickly you can resolve it inside of yourself when it happens. What's your recovery time? Do you hold on to the perceived hurt and tuck it away to use as ammunition at another time? Or do you use **forgiveness, grace,** and **humility** to lay down your arms and engage in dialogue rather than debate?

THE "Y" IN YOUR ROAD

Several months after our youngest son was born, we strapped him in a baby carrier and took our family hiking at Starved Rock State Park. As we followed the trails, there were several places where we paused at a Y in the trail. We talked with our kids about which direction we should go. Usually one way was more worn down than the other. Sometimes there were even deep ruts in the ground because one path had obviously been chosen more often than the other.

....

The same thing happens in marriage. As we hike through life together, we habitually respond in certain ways that form ruts in our mind. Without thinking, we'll head down the path of defensive familiarity following our well-worn footsteps. However, too often the path with ruts is "what we feel like doing" and the other path that's hardly been hiked is "what God wants us to do."

Stopping defensiveness requires us to push past our flesh (what we want to do) and seek out God (who will show us what we NEED to do). Galatians 5:16–17 (ESV) speaks to this: "But I say, walk by the Spirit, and you will not gratify the desires of the flesh. For the desires of the flesh are against the Spirit, and the desires of the Spirit are against the flesh, for these are opposed to each other, to keep you from doing the things you want to do."

So the question begs to be asked, "Am I going to do life and marriage my way or God's way?"

Just as our family paused at each Y and considered which route we would take, you and I have to pause and consider the options in front of us. Will we respond to our spouse's feedback with defensiveness that separates us, or will we put away our weapons and have a helpful dialogue that brings us together?

THE POWER OF FEEDBACK IN YOUR MARRIAGE

Defensiveness most often pops up when our spouse gives us some kind of feedback. We're not accustomed to using the word *feedback* in marriage. It's more often used in the workplace. Yet feedback is an important part of life. We need to know how our actions affect others, both positively and negatively. Kind, honest conversation fuels maturity and deepens intimacy.

Feedback in marriage is crucial, yet few of us do it well. We tend to respond with anger, defensiveness, blame, and shame. "Performance reviews" in marriage (giving feedback) allow us to recognize what is and isn't working.

Two types of feedback are healthy for marriage: responsive and reflective feedback. Let's look at why each is important and how to successfully give and receive feedback in marriage.

Responsive Feedback

Responsive feedback is what happens naturally every day in marriage. This is simply the way we respond to each other. It can be encouraging feedback like, "Wonderful dinner tonight, honey!" and "Wow, the yard looks wonderful!" Honestly, we all need to give more of this kind of feedback! Most of us are stingy with encouraging feedback. We're more tuned in to what our spouse doesn't do than what he or she does do. We could stand to crank it up two or three notches by simply noticing the little, often-taken-for-granted things our spouse does.

The other kind of responsive feedback is when we express frustration, hurt, or concern to each other. Too often we don't give this kind of feedback particularly well. When I (Mark) give feedback, I have two unhealthy tendencies and they are at the opposite ends of the spectrum. The first response is expressing frustration rather than communicating directly about how Jill's actions affect me. This often follows hinting—which, if you haven't figured it out, is never an effective form of communication.

My second tendency is to "stuff and blow." I tell myself it doesn't matter when really it does. I stuff it over and over, until I eventually blow. Raging, in case you also haven't figured it out, is never an effective form of communication either.

When I (Jill) give feedback in my marriage, my unhealthy tendency is to shoot so straight there's very little kindness and compassion. My factual approach clashes with Mark's emotional temperament. These days, I'm learning to speak with kindness and compassion in order for the message to be received better. Sometimes I take a deep breath to slow me down and give me time to consider *how* I'm giving my feedback.

While I (Mark) don't always get it right, these days I'm learning to speak up sooner, before I'm too frustrated to communicate clearly or keep my emotions in check. I intentionally speak with a calm voice of leadership that helps me stay emotionally steady. It's making a difference and I'm able to both give and receive feedback better.

While we were writing this chapter, Mark and our son Austin took off one evening for a bike ride. As the sun set, I (Jill) kept expecting them to ride into the driveway. When darkness fell, I texted Mark that I was very worried about them. He eventually responded that they were almost home. I was worried and my communication was loaded with anxiety, fear, and frustration. He could have easily given me a defensive response. Instead he disarmed my emotions with a caring, compassionate, gentle response.

It's okay to express frustration with one other. It's healthy and builds resiliency into the relationship. It's not the expressing of frustration but rather *the way* you express it that makes a difference in how it is received and how it impacts the relationship. The way we communicate our feelings needs to be intentional, though, being careful not to shame or punish our loved one with our tone or words. This is something I (Jill) have had to work on a lot. My tone can come across shaming, especially to a husband who already struggles with shame. I've not arrived yet, but I'm more often measuring the tone and the words I use.

It's also important that we keep a short leash on our frustrations. It requires courage to deal with them sooner rather than later. If we don't learn how to express our feelings and frustrations in healthy, direct, courageous ways, we'll end up dealing with them indirectly with sarcasm, snide remarks, teasing, inner resentment, and unfair grudges. These unhealthy responses move toward indifference and apathy, further separating us from each other.

When we're on the receiving side of our spouse's expressed frustration, the way we respond to that communication makes all the difference in the world. When receiving feedback, my (Mark's) unhealthy response is one of shame. My self-talk says, "I'm never enough." I don't just do bad things, I *am* bad . . . defective . . . and can never get it right. This is shame at its finest. My second unhealthy response is one of judgment toward Jill. I tell myself, "She is always critical. I can never make her happy." Neither of these responses is at all true.

When receiving feedback, my (Jill's) unhealthy response is blame. My self-talk is clouded in pride that says, "I'm not the only one with a problem here." Or, "I'm not wrong, just misunderstood." The only way to turn these puppies around is with **humility**. These days I'm letting Mark know he's been heard by repeating back to him what he's said. This allows me to let his words soak in and gives me a way to respond that isn't filled with blame. I may not agree with all the feedback, but with humility as the lens I'm seeing the feedback through, God shows me what part is true and needs to be addressed.

For me (Mark), I'm working at standing firm in who I am in Christ. When the old messages start to play in my head, I replace them with the truth I know. I recognize the ploy of the enemy to whisper those lies and I've stopped playing into his hand. This allows me to hear Jill's communication and recognize the value of what she is saying. I may not agree with all of the feedback, but I'm asking God to show me what I need to hear and own.

Most of our defensive responses occur because we're formulating a response in our mind rather than listening to what is being said. We actually can learn to silence that constant stream of counterarguments going on in our mind. It requires us to take the other Y in the road—the one less traveled. The destination is definitely worth the effort but requires us to learn how to dial down defensiveness. Here are four steps to stop defensiveness in yourself:

(1) *Receive what's being communicated.* You might even say, "I hear what you're saying. Let me think on it a bit." You don't have to respond more than that, as long as you can commit to truly think and pray about what was communicated and return to your spouse with a genuine response.

It's the "returning" part that gets most of us in trouble. We think, *If I don't bring it up again, he/she will just forget about it.* Don't do it! Your integrity is at stake and your return to the communication builds trust in your relationship. When Jill and I have hard conversations, I (Mark) always feel that I have a CD spinning in my head that can't land on a song. I need some time to think about what was said. However, I have learned that I have to be a man of my word when I ask for some time to think about what she has communicated.

(2) *Start your response with "What I hear you saying is . . ." and repeat back what they communicated to you.* Just as with handling disagreement, this helps your spouse feel heard, regardless of whether you agree with him or her or not. It opens you to dialogue and keeps you from falling into debate.

(3) *Ask yourself if you are responding in an old way.* Maybe your parent never let you have your own opinions. Your spouse isn't your parent, but this situation feels similar. Be careful not to impose your feelings from a previous situation onto the current situation. In the moment it may look, feel, and smell similar, but this is a different person standing in front of you and they need a different response than the knee-jerk one you want to give.

(4) *Measure your words with an appropriate response.* If you were wrong, apologize and ask for forgiveness. If your spouse has brought up a good point but needs some additional perspective, after letting him or her know they've been heard, continue with, "Here's some perspective that might be helpful . . ."

Marriage is a lifetime job. It's one we're constantly learning about. Our spouse is usually the best person to give us feedback, but we have to make sure we're emotionally healthy in how we both give and receive feedback. The more each of us is tuned in to where growth is needed, the more we are addressing our unhealthy lenses. When we address unhealthy lenses, we replace conflict with conversation and our marriage is strengthened.

Reflective Feedback

Reflective feedback might be likened to what happens when a business or organization steps away from the everyday, goes off-site, and both evaluates how they're doing and makes plans for the future. Few of us engage in this kind of feedback in our marriage, but doing so can help us look at relationship patterns, set goals, and dream and plan for our future together.

Set aside some time to just talk about your marriage as well as becoming familiar with each other's hopes and dreams. You can even tackle some of these topics on a road trip you take together. In fact, *Love and Respect* author Emerson Eggerichs recommends doing just that. He says women like to speak face-to-face, while men prefer shoulder to shoulder: in a car, on the couch, out to eat, or at your own dinner table. Even washing dishes or pulling weeds side by side will often net more communication than a face-to-face conversation ever will.

We recently asked each other some of these questions as we were driving. I (Jill) learned that Mark has an Alaskan cruise on his bucket list. I. Had. No. Idea!

See what you can discover with some of these conversation starters:

Name two things on your personal bucket list.
If you had to give our marriage a grade, what grade would you give it?
What could we do to improve that grade?

What is weighing heavy on your heart that I can be praying for you about?

How is our pace of life? Too fast? Not active enough?

How are we doing at exercising? Is there anything we could do together?

Are there any adjustments on the home front we need to make? Division of chores? Parenting challenges? Meals? Laundry? Housekeeping? Yard?

Are we satisfied with the time we have together as a couple? What do we need to do to change that?

What is the most important goal you have for yourself for the coming year?

What is the most important goal you have for us for the coming year?

What do I do that you'd like me to do more often?

What do I do that you'd like me to do less often?

How are we doing financially? Is there anything we need to change in how we're managing our money?

How are we doing spiritually? Are we serving in our church and community in meaningful ways that match our passions? Are we growing in our faith? Is there anything we can do to grow together in our faith? Can we pray or read the Bible together in a new or different way?

How do you feel about your career?

What can I do to help you achieve your goals?

What would you like our life to look like in five years? Ten years? Twenty years?

How are we doing with extended family relationships? Are there any boundaries we need to set or reinforce? Do we need to make plans to see family more often or less often?

. . . .

What do you like best about our holiday traditions?
What do you like least about our holiday traditions?
What activities would you like us to do more often?
What activities would you like us to do less often?
What does your ideal vacation look like?
What could we do to celebrate our next anniversary?
How do you prefer to celebrate your next birthday?
Is there something special we'd like to do for our upcoming milestone anniversary? Should we start planning or saving toward that?

HONEST CONVERSATIONS

Some of the biggest blocks to honest conversations are defensive responses. Because of this, defensiveness hinders intimacy. It shuts down communication, forcing us each to our own corners.

The slow fade of defensiveness moves from unresolved conflict to isolation. We "lick our wounds" privately and internally rationalize why we are right. Too often we don't seek to understand.

We can turn this around with courage, humility, forgiveness, and grace. **Courage** helps us to speak up and give our spouse direct, responsive feedback when we're frustrated. Partnered with **humility**, courage also allows us to dig deep and identify places where we need to pause at the Y in the road and blaze new trails in how we respond. Most importantly, **forgiveness** and **grace** keep our hearts from getting cluttered and piled up with resentment. They allow us to lay down our arms and move from debate to dialogue. This keeps our heart open and available to the God we serve and the one we love.

· · · · · · · ·

⊹ THINK ABOUT IT ⊹

Where are you most defensive in your marriage? Have you seen defensiveness fade into unresolved issues, isolation, and even disengagement? Are you ready to take a step to turn that around as much as it depends upon you?

Examine your self-talk in regards to your marriage. Begin paying attention to the negative thoughts you have about your spouse or your marriage. Begin replacing the negative thoughts with positive thoughts.

⊹ TALK ABOUT IT ⊹

My biggest takeaway from this chapter was_____
_____

When it comes to responsive feedback, I can see that my default response is usually _____
_____

Let's ask each other three of the reflective questions today.

⊹ TALK TO GOD ABOUT IT ⊹

God, I confess that I'm not always the best at receiving feedback from _____. I want to listen to learn and resist the urge to formulate a defensive response in my head. Help me to see when my reasons threaten to trample relationship. Help me to increase my positive feedback, and show me how to give negative feedback, lovingly and sparingly. Keep me growing in You, Lord. Help me to respond the way You want me to instead of the way I feel like doing. In Jesus' Name. Amen.

Today's Truth: "But the Helper, the Holy Spirit, whom the Father will send in my name, he will teach you all things and bring to your remembrance all that I have said to you."
JOHN 14:26 (ESV)

## CHAPTER 9

BEWARE THE *Quicksand*

THE SLOW FADE OF NAÏVETÉ

*T*he young mom chatted with me after the Hearts at Home conference where more than five thousand moms had gathered for a wonderful weekend of laughter, encouragement, and education for the challenging job of being a mom. "Have you ever thought about having a conference for dads?" she asked.

Before I could reply, she continued, "There's a stay-at-home dad in our neighborhood and he's become my best friend. We take the kids to the park together, shop together, and even do our once-a-month cooking together. He's a great guy!" She continued to chat, but my unspoken thoughts now overshadowed her spoken words.

Sirens, whistles, and red flags were going off inside my head. I wanted to scream, "No! Don't be naïve. Remove the blinders! Please put some boundaries in place and build a hedge of protection around your marriage!" It was obvious she had no idea about the danger of this seemingly harmless situation.

Naïveté is to knowingly place ourselves in a position of relational danger downplaying the possibility that it could lead to compromise. Years ago, that primarily meant being careful about not being alone with someone of the opposite sex other than your spouse. Today, social media has opened up a whole new arena of relationship circles where seemingly innocent connections can lead to not-so-innocent relationships.

Mark and I spend countless hours each month mentoring hurting marriages. We counsel others based on our own "back from the brink" experience when naïveté set the fade in motion, infidelity occurred, and our own marriage seemed hopeless. Many of the couples we meet with are also dealing with damage caused by infidelity. The story is the same every time: the unfaithful spouse develops a relationship that started innocently. It was someone to talk to, someone who listened and cared. In most of those stories, naïveté allowed the interaction to happen in the first place. Then the fade began.

Here's our story:

Mark: I'll be the first to confess that for most of our marriage Jill has always been very intentional about making advance decisions to protect our marriage. While I accommodated her requests to a certain extent, deep down I felt in control and that "rules" were ridiculous. As I write those words, I think of their foolishness. I also think of quicksand, which has the appearance of the ground or terrain being normal and safe. Yet when an individual steps on quicksand, the person begins to sink. It is the same with naïveté. I hate that it took a tragedy for me to realize how foolish I had been in resisting wisdom and not putting boundaries in place to protect myself and my marriage.

Jill: My commitment to keeping temptation at bay came from a situation I experienced early in our marriage. We'd been married five years and had two children. Mark was in Bible college and I was doing day care during the day and working at a dinner theater several evenings a week. Mark and I were meeting each other coming and going, and before I knew it, I was enjoying the conversations I was having and the attention I was getting from a man I worked with at the theater. Temptation set in and I realized the dangerous place my head and my heart were in. Thankfully I got honest with Mark, quit the job, and from that point on, established predetermined boundaries in place to keep temptation at bay.

Our human nature has a way of remembering what we need to forget and forgetting what we need to remember.

Mark: I remember the night Jill confessed to me her attraction to her coworker. Amazingly, I handled the conversation well. I was so glad she was being honest. We both talked about what steps we needed to take to get her out of this place of temptation, including upping the investment in our own marriage. If only I could have kept this situation at the forefront of my mind so many years later when I faced my own temptation. Our human nature, however, has a way of remembering what we need to forget and forgetting what we need to remember.

Twenty-three years later, as I was nearing my fiftieth birthday, my inner life took a nosedive. In all areas of my life: in ministry, in my job, in my marriage, and with God, I didn't feel like I was "good enough."

It felt like I was falling short in every relationship I had. I was disappointed, frustrated, burned out. I had left pastoring so Jill and I could do ministry more closely, and even that didn't feel like it was working out as I imagined it would. I was angry and came to the conclusion that the only answer I could figure out to stop that feeling was to be done with it all.

I was done trying to be what everyone wanted. I was done trying to be what Jill wanted. I was done being what God wanted. It was all impossible, and I was a man without hope. To be naïve when you have so much turmoil going on inside of yourself is even more dangerous and volatile. Eventually I moved from innocent conversations, to an emotional affair, to a physical affair. I postured myself to leave my marriage and start a new life. I told myself the kids would be okay. They would be resilient. They would survive. I had already secretly set up an apartment weeks before. I walked out the door feeling free, but I would later come to realize it was a false sense of freedom. You see, I was leaving, but I was still taking me with me.

Jill: I knew that Mark was struggling, but I had no idea the turmoil going on inside his head and his heart. Without self-imposed guardrails in place, social media opened the door for the beginnings of an illicit relationship.

Mark: My naïveté fade started with "this won't hurt anyone" (**naïve**) to "I deserve this. I need to let off some steam" (**rationalize**) to "another relationship just might be the answer" (**compromise**). This is a real-life picture of James 1:14–15 (ESV): "But each person is tempted when he is lured and enticed by his own desire. Then desire when it has conceived gives birth to sin, and sin when it is fully grown brings forth death." My misplaced desire led to sin, which led to death. Not a physical death, but emotional, spiritual, and relational death.

Jill: We stop naïveté with **wisdom**. First Corinthians 13:7 says that love "protects." It is our job to protect our marriage. These days I'm as committed as ever to the wisdom of accountability. If I need to go to a business meeting or a business lunch with a man, I ask someone else to come along. As the emails have come in from both men and women whose relationships are hurting, only Mark is responding to the ones from men, and I am responding to the ones from women.

Mark: These days I'm embracing wisdom. I'm a contractor who is often in people's homes during the day. I work hard to make sure I have another crew member with me while working in someone's home. When I'm traveling, I ask a friend to travel with me. I'm also no longer on Facebook. I'll admit that I miss it, but my family is too important to me to risk the temptation. When I disregarded healthy guardrails for the lure of Facebook, I was not accepting wisdom that I had been given for protecting my marriage. There is an enemy that is out to steal and destroy. He tickles our flesh into temptations that become decisions of devastation. Engage wisdom, protect your marriage, and be reminded of who the real enemy is.

SOUL MIRAGES

We've all seen them on a hot day. Up ahead, it looks like there's a sheet of water on the road. As we get closer, we realize there's no water there at all. It's a mirage caused by the heat mixed with light in just the right way.

We've all experienced soul mirages in some way. We tell ourselves, "In the fall when all my kids are in school, I'm going to get all the closets cleaned out." Or, "Next month, I'm going to sit down face-to-face with my spouse for a few minutes every night after the kids are in bed." Or, "When we got married, I knew I'd found my soulmate. What happened?" Or, "I'm done with this relationship. I'm going to pursue this other person because we're made for each other."

These mirages are really illusions. They appear real, they seem possible, but in real life they actually don't exist or can't happen the way we ideally hoped. Soul mirages are the lies we tell ourselves. Some soul mirages are true fantasies—they don't exist—and others are simply unrealistic expectations—things that exist but not to the level we are expecting in our mind.

Soul mirages are a part of the slow fade of naïveté. They set us up for disappointment, contribute to our tendency to rationalize, and too often lead the way to compromise. As I (Mark) shared earlier, I tend to have a lot of idealism inside of me. When unrealistic expectations linked arms with naïveté, I was in trouble and desperately needed to get out my God-tools. I wish I had five years ago. Yet you can bet I do now.

I will never forget the look on my youngest son's face when I told him that I was leaving. The look of shock, horror, devastation, and betrayal still haunts me when I think about it today. You see, I'd told myself a lie—I believed a soul mirage—that my children would be okay if I left. I told myself they would understand. Here's some perspective from our oldest daughter, Anne:

I picked up the phone thinking it was any ordinary call from my dad. We chatted for a minute and then he dropped the news on me. It was a quick conversation. He shared that he had moved out and if I had any questions he would be happy to answer them later but that he needed to call my siblings now. He didn't mention the affair at all. He just shared he was "done."

Mom called me a few minutes later and we just cried. She asked me if Dad had shared the reason why he had left, to which I shared the reasons he gave me. She then said, "I've given him the opportunity to be honest with you and I can't protect him anymore." She then shared about the other relationship. I was sick to my stomach. My family had always been a source of stability and that was crashing around me.

Honestly, we kids had known for a while that Dad was struggling. He was just off. We'd often talk about how Dad was no longer the same. My dad has always been caring, wise, and discerning. He was the one I would turn to if I wanted to be heard or think through things. But he was no longer these things consistently. He was distant and distracted. While we knew he was struggling with life, we had no idea the magnitude of it all.

I struggled with my role in all of this. I was married and pregnant with my second child. I lived four hours away. I was removed from the situation, but the disappointment and tears were still the same.

The following weekend, all of the siblings came home. It was beyond strange, sad and hard. A piece was missing in the house. And not just that, my daughter Rilyn, who was almost two at the time, was very confused. She kept asking, "Where's Pappaw?" How does one answer that to a two-year-old? I was angry that my dad put us in the position to have to deal with the aftermath . . . not only ours but our child's as well.

Matt and I asked my dad to meet and talk. (Can I just say that I hated having to schedule time with my dad?) Never have I prayed so fervently for someone. I kept asking God, "What do I do here? Do I call him out on stuff? Or do I just love him through it?" I was so nervous and anxious. How was I supposed to act in this situation? As soon as I gave him a hug, I knew that I needed to be straightforward and honest with him. I was so grateful for the peace God gave me entering into this conversation.

I shared with him that I still loved him but was disappointed and hurt. The more we talked, the more evident it was that the man I sat across from was not my dad. This man was tired, hardened, skewed, and selfish. And while he thought this new relationship and new life was the answer, I knew that wasn't the case.

As the conversation wrapped up, I shared that ultimately we still wanted relationship with him. I still wanted my children to see and know my dad through this all. But, it was going to be with some boundaries, which included us not going to his new apartment and being cautious with Rilyn. We scheduled a time for him to come to the house to see Rilyn the next day. That interaction was hard. It was hard to see my dad walk into his own house as a guest. It was hard to have to say hello and good-bye in such a short time. It was hard to explain this all to Rilyn. . . . "Why is Pappaw leaving?" It was hard to watch my dad hug Rilyn goodbye with tears in his eyes. This was all just really hard.

Three of us were married and lived away from home. Two of my broth-ers still lived at home. For me, I was able to separate myself a little bit because of distance. I can't imagine the emotions my brothers felt. I can't speak for my other siblings, but for me, it was still incredibly difficult to journey through this as an adult child.

Five years later, I am so grateful for the choices my dad has made. He chose God. He chose my mom. He chose family. The midlife crisis certainly took its toll on all of our family relationships. I would say we are much more aware of relational dynamics now. It certainly has made me more aware of that in my own marriage. More than anything, I've learned that love is more than a feeling—it's a series of choices and commitment.

Just reading Anne's words is very hard for me (Mark). I wish with my whole heart that I'd made different choices and that I had handled my challenges differently. I'm grateful for how God has redeemed the brokenness I caused in our family. I now know, however, that my determination that Jill and I were just "too incompatible," that "this new relationship will be better," and that "the kids will be fine," were all soul mirages. They were lies from the enemy that I believed hook, line, and sinker.

BUILDING HEDGES

We have a line of trees along the west side of our country home. The previous owners wisely planted the trees to provide a hedge of protection against the winds that gust across the cornfields of central Illinois. Those trees serve as a visual picture of another hedge of protection we need to plant in our lives: a hedge of protection around our marriage.

On the day we say, "I do," we fully intend to fulfill every promise we make. But marriage is hard work, and our feelings ebb and flow with the ups and downs of life. When our life is fast paced, or our spouse is less attentive, or our marriage is placed on the back burner of life, we can easily slip into a mode where we begin to think that maybe "the grass is greener on the other side of the fence."

No marriage is immune from temptation. Hedges are advance decisions we make to protect our marriage. They keep temptation at bay, stop naïveté, and keep the marriage relationship a top priority. Let's look at some specific hedges we all need to plant around our marriage.

Hedge #1: Stay clear of unnecessarily spending time with someone of the opposite sex. For instance, if you are interested in securing the services of a personal trainer at the local gym, choose someone of the same sex. You're simply being wise to not put yourself in a place where you're consistently alone with someone of the opposite sex. Many an affair has started with the "harmless" act of enjoying an evening jog together. If your spouse can't participate in the activity with you, do it alone, with a friend of the same sex, with a group, or not at all.

What if you had a friendship with someone of the opposite sex before you got married? Then spend time together in family settings. When you said, "I do," your spouse and protecting your marriage took a higher priority than your pre-marriage friendship. If I (Jill) have to text, email, or call another man for any reason, I let Mark know. Recently Mark hired a female home designer for his remodeling business. He came to me first and talked about hedges he was putting in place. When our kids were little, I, rather than Mark, drove babysitters home. All of these advance decisions have nothing to do with insecurity in our relationship. They protect our hearts and those of people of the opposite sex with whom we come into contact.

Hedge #2: Share carefully. If you find yourself sharing things about your marriage or yourself that you haven't or wouldn't share with your spouse, that's a red flag to warn you to turn away from the relationship rather than toward it. Not all affairs are physical — an emotional affair is

. . . .

as damaging as a physical affair. The more we share and begin to console each other, the more we begin to build an emotional bond. While the shared sympathy feels like needed comfort, it becomes a dangerous slope that can lead to a surprising mutual attraction. Then what once was a difficult marriage becomes an unbearable one in the contrast of newly discovered intimacy and attraction.

Hedge #3: Stay in large, public settings. Determine not to meet one-on-one with anyone of the opposite sex, even in the workplace. If your coworker of the opposite sex asks if he or she can join you for lunch, ask a third person to join you as well. If necessary, share the boundary you and your spouse have agreed upon in your marriage. You just might lead by example.

Hedge #4: Don't be naïve. Most people who end up in affairs don't set out to have an affair. Infidelity usually begins with an innocent relationship with someone of the opposite sex that, in time, moves to an emotional depth that draws us to cross a line of fidelity. Fades happen in marriage. Not understanding the reality of those feelings and not doing anything about them is naïve.

Hedge #5: Increase your investment at home. No marriage is designed to last a lifetime if left on the back burner. Solid marriages are built by spending time together, laughing together, and playing together. If you are not currently dating your mate, set up dates for the coming months and make spending time together a priority. Then *stick to your plan*! Lots of "urgent" needs will come up. Don't take the bait!

There's nothing more urgent than protecting your marriage.

Too many parents are also naïve about investing in their marriage when the kids are little. Admittedly, it's a hassle to arrange childcare and often there's not a lot of extra in the budget for "dates" or paying a sitter. However, tending to your marriage is just as important as tending to your children. Taking care of your marriage is one of the best parenting strategies available to you. Don't be naïve in thinking that you will take time for the two of you after the kids leave. There may not be much of a relationship for you to invest in if you wait that long.

Hedge #6: Step into your spouse's world. Mark loves it when I (Jill) stop by and see the remodeling work he's doing on a job. I love it when he goes with me to a speaking engagement. I'm not particularly interested in remodeling, but I am interested in my husband. My hubby has heard me speak hundreds of times and he could definitely be doing something else than joining me for another trip. However, he chooses to stay engaged in my world as a way of investing and protecting our marriage.

Hedge #7: Add fun to your relationship. Mark once told me (Jill) that I was a terrible flirt. He particularly likes to flirt by text. I admit I was terrible at it until I discovered the Bitmoji app! It's a free app on my smartphone that allows me to send graphics to my hubby that look like me and say fun things like "Thinking of you!" and "You're hot!" and "Can't wait to see you!" (Disclaimer: it's not a Christian app and occasionally some of the graphics contain a spicy word or two.) It's definitely been a game changer for flirting for me!

You can also tuck a note in his lunch box, send her on a scavenger

....

hunt for love notes you've written, call him over lunch, send her a quick text that simply says, "I'm thinking of you!" Remember sometimes the little things are really the big things and fun in marriage is a little thing that really can make a big difference!

Hedge #8: Share temptation with your spouse. Along the same lines, make sure you're safe for your spouse to share temptations with. If you explode with anger or emotion when your spouse communicates a struggle, you'll shut the door on future honest conversation. The night I (Jill) shared with Mark about my attraction to my coworker, he stayed calm and asked questions. I was so grateful. There's something powerful that happens when we move our temptation from the darkness into the light. It often removes the draw of the temptation. In darkness, the temptation grows. When we shine the light on it by admitting it, it slows or completely stops the growth of feelings. One couple I (Jill) know chose not to pursue a friendship with another couple because the wife found the husband of the other couple attractive and simply didn't want that temptation. She was honest, and he made it safe for her to be honest. Thankfully he didn't take her communication personally, and they decided together it was best not to pursue that friendship.

Hedge #9: No secrets. There's never a good reason to keep a secret from your spouse. No secrets about where the money goes, where you've been, and what's really going on in your head and your heart. If you're hiding something, that should be a red flag that something needs to change. Honesty and vulnerability are essential in protecting your marriage.

Hedge #10: Watch for seasons of increased vulnerability. I (Jill) remember when my friend Becky said to me about two weeks after Mark left, "Jill, you need to be very careful. You're in a vulnerable place emotionally and you have to make sure you don't get drawn into temptation yourself now that you're alone." I'm so thankful for her wise words. It wasn't but two hours later when I got on Facebook and an old high school boyfriend reached out to me. If you think that's coincidence, think again. That's spiritual warfare and I wasn't about to play into the enemy's hands.

Has your spouse been ill? On the road a lot? Have you been dealing with a crisis in your family? These are all places where you're tired, maybe discouraged, and likely feeling a little disconnected from your spouse because of life's circumstances. These are high vulnerability times when you need to turn up the heat in your own marriage.

Hedge #11: Pay attention to your thought-life. When all you think about is your spouse's faults, any other man or woman will certainly look better. If you find yourself entertaining destructive thoughts about your spouse, work to turn that around. Make a list of the strengths that initially attracted you to your mate. Increase the encouragement and decrease the criticism you give to your spouse.

Hedge #12: Don't play the comparison game. We are all human. We all make mistakes, have bad habits and annoying behaviors. When we compare a "new friend" to our spouse, it's an unfair comparison because we are not seeing them in a "living under the same roof, taking care of kids at 3 a.m., struggling to make ends meet" reality. Refrain

....

from making unfair comparisons. This is where we have to come face-to-face with our soul mirages that aren't telling us the truth.

Hedge #13: Communicate your needs to your spouse. In one of my (Mark's) customers' homes, the book *Fifty Shades of Grey* was sitting on her coffee table. I commented on the book and she said to me in all innocence, "Mark, deep down every woman wants to be led. Everyone thinks this book is all about sex, but it's really all about leadership." She went on to say that "women get tired of leading and carrying all of the weight. I am drawn to the man who leads." I was very surprised at her take on the book. But it still fell in the naïveté category, as she was naïvely using a fictional story to feed her own inner craving for her husband to lead. I wondered if she had ever communicated that craving directly to her husband. When we communicate directly rather than working to get our needs met in a roundabout way, we're actually putting a hedge around our marriage. Even if our spouse doesn't respond in a positive way, we can know we did the right thing by communicating.

Hedge #14: Push transparent, thoughtful, accountable communication to your spouse. It's not a sign of a lack of trust for married couples to check in with each other—it's an act of kindness and an effort of intentionality. Your spouse is always on a "need to know" status, and he or she needs to know what you're doing. If you're going to be late, call and let your spouse know. If you're going to stop by the store on the way home, shoot your spouse a quick text to say so. When we find out about these things later, it can cause us to feel left out or to be frustrated because, "If I'd known you were going to the store, I would have had you pick up razor blades. I used the last one this morning!" Communication is a courtesy to your spouse but also keeps your emotional intimacy a priority.

Hedge #15: Stay away from pornography and erotic movies and novels. Viewing pornography is an affair in and of itself. Soft porn in the form of erotic novels and even some R-rated movies can be equally dangerous. Porn draws our mind away from our spouse. It sets up unrealistic expectations. It erodes contentment. Porn is addictive and can become an idol in our life. When I have struggled with porn in different seasons of my marriage, it has fueled my discontent and put unrealistic expectations on Jill. Sex was not good enough, frequent enough, or anything enough when porn was setting the standard.

Men are drawn to pornography because of our own inner drive and need to be wanted. They crave for the woman to seek them, to want them, to need them, to be available for them. This craving for men becomes a fantasy that causes a creeping separateness in marriage that increases over time. Pursuing porn and believing it won't hurt anyone is very naïve. (Mark's note: if porn is a huge issue in your life, consider attending an Every Man's Battle workshop. I did and found it very helpful! www.newlife.com/emb.)

Hedge #16: Watch what you feed your mind. Some couples make an advance decision not to watch any movie that has infidelity in the story line. Others choose not to watch R-rated movies that are rated R for sexual content.

. . . .

Years ago, I (Jill) watched the movie *The Bridges of Madison County*. Set in 1965, the movie tells the story of Francesca (Meryl Streep), a mom who is unfulfilled in her marriage. While her husband and kids are away for a few days, she meets a photographer, Robert (Clint Eastwood). Robert stops and asks for directions to the local covered bridges he hopes to photograph. She decides to take him to the bridges herself. They talk and share their lives, and eventually carry on a four-day affair. In ways that only movies can, there was the implication that before the affair Francesca's life was black and white and after the affair it was in color. I was home alone because Mark was out of town and our marriage was in a hard season. I remember after watching the movie, the rationalizing thoughts that entered my mind: *Well, her husband didn't pay attention to her. She deserved a little bit of love.* Then I caught myself and realized what I was doing. I determined then and there that I had to be careful about what I chose to watch and read.

Many of us are naïve about the books that we read and the movies we watch and how they affect us. We innocently pick up a book or pick out a movie for entertainment purposes, not realizing that these stories can easily cause or fuel discontent in our marriage. Romantic sex scenes in movies or books can cause us to think, *It's not that way in my marriage.* Suddenly our normal, real marriage is compared to a vivid, maybe glamorized, but fictionalized account of another relationship, and it doesn't measure up.

Hedge #17: Watch who you spend time with. If you spend large amounts of time with someone who is critical of his or her spouse, you'll be affected. If you have a friend who is a flirt, you'll be affected. If you spend a lot of time with someone who doesn't live life God's way, it will affect you. We need to be lights to a dark world, so this hedge isn't about not interacting with nonbelievers. It is, however, a call to ask yourself if your friendship with this person is good for your marriage or not.

Hedge #18: Seek truth. We live in an "anything goes" world; what's "right" is relative to how we feel. That's not the way God created things to be. He gave us His Word to spell out right and wrong—not to limit us, but to protect us!

Keep reading the Bible. Wisdom counters naïveté. The Bible is full of wisdom that we desperately need to saturate ourselves with. Our goal needs to be to become more like Jesus every day. The only way we can do that is to spend time with Him and learn more about the upside-down, sometimes unpopular decisions He made when He lived on this earth.

Hedge #19: Love and respect around the clock. If you wouldn't say it or wouldn't say it with that tone in public, then don't say it or say it that way at home. We're usually on our best behavior when we're around other people. God doesn't tell us to love when we feel like it. He doesn't say that respect is optional and only when our spouse gets things right. He tells us to love and respect each other, period. This small but important hedge protects our spouse's tender heart.

Hedge #20: Install an Internet filter. You don't have to go looking for temptation; these days you can stumble upon it very easily. Don't be naïve. Install an Internet filter to keep the stumbling from happening to you or your kids. We've used K9 Web Protection the most (www.k9webprotection.com), installing it on all of our computers. It's also available for smartphones though we've personally never used it that way. We're also familiar with Covenant Eyes. This is accountability software where you have a friend or your spouse receive a copy of your Internet history on a regular basis.

One husband we know who struggled with being drawn to pornography decided to remove the web browser from his smartphone. And while we're talking about technology, passwords should never be kept from each other. If you have something you don't want your spouse to see, it's probably a red flag that you shouldn't be involved in it. Both partners in a marriage should be completely comfortable with having their spouse look at any social media accounts, text messages, emails, or other forms of communication. These are all wise decisions to keep temptation at bay.

Hedge #21: Seek help. Seek encouragement even in the good times. Find someone today—a Christian counselor, an older married couple— you can talk to about the little things today. If your marriage is struggling, the answer isn't another relationship. Seeking help is a sign of strength, not weakness. A mentor or Christian counselor who will honor your values regarding marriage and commitment can provide valuable perspective and help set new strategies for a marriage that can go the distance.

God's Word tells us that "each person is tempted when he is lured and enticed by his own desire. Then desire when it has conceived gives birth to sin, and sin when it is fully grown brings forth death" (James

1:14–15 ESV). Temptation, enticement, desire, sin, death: those are the steps infidelity takes. Because of that, we have to put boundaries in place that keep us from stepping into situations where step one — temptation — can take place.

When the hedge of trees was planted on our property, each tree was planted individually. As the trees grew in size and strength, they worked together to protect our home from the unpredictable weather and wind. Each hedge that we plant around our marriage will do the same. Each time we make one advance decision to protect our marriage, we are taking an important step to build a marriage that is marked by faithfulness and on its way to lasting a lifetime.

GET OUT YOUR TOOLBOX

I (Mark) listened as Todd (not his real name) shared about his own marriage and confessed an affair he had that went on for many months. As an outside salesman for a large company, he travels quite a bit for his job. When he said that opportunities for infidelity were everywhere on the road, I asked him what boundaries he had now put in place to safeguard his marriage and himself. His first response was how embarrassing that would be to put limits or boundaries upon himself when traveling. I found his response interesting, because he had just been crying over his affair and yet he wasn't willing to put boundaries in place. Todd needed **courage**. He needed to be willing to be called "old-fashioned" or even "ridiculous" for the sake of his marriage. He needed to be willing to stand up to peer pressure from other on-the-road sales reps. Doing the right thing isn't always easy.

For me, my unwillingness to put boundaries in place was full-on pride. I had believed that I could do whatever I wanted without any potential compromise. I rationalized that I was strong enough. I was mature enough. I wouldn't be affected. I didn't need boundaries. Like Todd, I thought, *What would people think?* And that, my friend, is pride.

"I can do this on my own!" Yes, that is pride too.

"No one else does this!" Pride again.

I had so much pride coursing through me, and I needed to get rid of it. But I hadn't honestly realized it was pride. You see, I mistook my thoughts and decisions as confidence. For most of my life, I lacked confidence. In not feeling like I "was enough," my self-esteem suffered. This fed my passivity. Suddenly I was standing on my own two feet. I was making my own way. I was telling myself, "I'm done with the old life and I'm taking control and moving on." It felt like I was experiencing confidence for the first time in a long time. What I was experiencing, however, was pride camouflaged as confidence. What's the difference?

Pride never says, "I'm sorry." Confidence says, "I'm sorry. Will you please forgive me?"

Pride isolates and doesn't accept input. Confidence seeks the wisdom of others.

Pride bristles when correction is given. Confidence welcomes feedback.

Pride says, "I know the way." Confidence says, "God knows the way."

Pride says, "I'm doing things my way." Confidence says, "I'm doing things God's way."

Pride says, "Look at me." Confidence says, "Look what God is doing!"

Pride is rooted in lies. Confidence is rooted in truth.

God says it best in Proverbs 11:2: "When pride comes, then comes disgrace, but with the humble is wisdom." And Proverbs 16:18: "Pride goes before destruction, and a haughty spirit before a fall" (both ESV). We desperately need **humility** to demolish the stronghold of pride in our heart.

Wisdom is the third tool needed to address naïveté. Another word for naïveté is foolishness. I think of countless stories where men I (Mark) have mentored have said, "I was so naïve," or "I was so foolish. I didn't mean for it to come to this!" Building hedges, tackling soul mirages, and staying steady requires wisdom.

Today, I (Mark) am experiencing real confidence as I keep my eyes on Jesus. It doesn't mean life is easy or even easier. Just this week I have faced some huge challenges as a business owner. The old Mark would have been off to the races believing lies and chasing mirages. The new Mark is working to stay steady with humility, wisdom, and courage.

We can be naïve about every one of the fades we've explored: unrealistic expectations, disagreement, defensiveness, minimizing, and not accepting. We start with one emotion or thought that we feel is harmless. Then we rationalize it, and before we realize it, we've slid right into compromise. We can't let our guard down when it comes to protecting our marriage!

Protect your heart from wandering by not putting yourself in situations of opportunity. Protect your mind from temptation by choosing what you watch and read. Protect your family from heartbreak by staying focused on your marriage and your family. Whatever you give your energy to is what will grow, heal, and flourish. Give your marriage your best

. . . .

investment—not your leftovers. First Corinthians 13:7 says love protects. Commit today to protect your heart, your mind, and your marriage.

❖ THINK ABOUT IT ❖

What about you? Is there anywhere you are being naïve in your marriage? Are you rationalizing? A little too close to compromising? What "soul mirages" are you chasing? Where do you need to apply humility, courage, or wisdom today?

❖ TALK ABOUT IT ❖

My biggest takeaway from this chapter was_____

_____

Looking at the hedges listed in this chapter, the five that are most important to me right now are_____

_____

When it comes to naïveté, I realize that I most need to use my tool of _____

_____

❖ TALK TO GOD ABOUT IT ❖

Lord, I confess that I'm naïve and haven't taken protecting my marriage seriously. Where I want to rationalize, help me to value wisdom. Where I'm afraid of being made fun of for setting boundaries, give me courage. Where I don't want to make the extra effort to do the right thing, give me humility to know that I'm not immune to temptation. Show me how to steer clear of temptation. When I'm faced with it, help me to run in the opposite direction. More than anything, show me how to keep fertilizing the grass in my own yard. In Jesus' Name. Amen.

Today's Truth: "Watch and pray that you may not enter into temptation. The spirit indeed is willing, but the flesh is weak." MATTHEW 26:41 (ESV)

## CHAPTER 10

NAKED BUT NOT *Ashamed*

THE SLOW FADE OF AVOIDING EMOTION

*I*n the field of home remodeling, fairly expensive tools allow you to gather information from inside walls. Based upon thermal imaging technology, one can see where heat is escaping due to a lack of insulation. These instruments also help you locate wiring and pipes inside walls. Obviously, this is a huge help when remodeling.

Wouldn't it be simpler in marriage if there were a similar tool we could use to gather information about each other? We could simply scan our spouse and see all the experiences, memories, emotions, thoughts, temperament, and personality traits that make up the person he or she is. Of course that doesn't exist and even if you could scan and get information, it wouldn't mean nearly as much as being able to talk

. . . .

through it. Interestingly though, one of the best definitions of intimacy we've ever heard is "into-me-see." Sounds a bit like that remodeling tool, doesn't it?

A guarded heart causes disconnect and emotional distance. We have to learn to be open, honest, and vulnerable with our spouse, uncovering our deepest thoughts and feelings. Depending on how emotions were handled in our family of origin, we may have some work to do in this area. Here's our story:

Mark: Because I'm a feeler, I always longed for a deeper emotional connection with Jill. I wanted to know her inside and out, comfort her when she was sad, reassure her when she felt insecure, and encourage her when she was down. I wanted her to *need* me to do all those things.

Jill: I've always been strong, independent, steady, and secure. I rarely need anything—emotionally or physically (yes, that probably has something to do with why I was still content with my green gingham wallpaper in our kitchen for nearly twenty years). As a thinker, I wasn't particularly emotional. In fact, I wasn't real "in tune" with my feelings at all. They didn't guide my thinking. They didn't help me make decisions. I believed deep down that feelings didn't matter. Only facts mattered.

Mark and I started alternating how we used our counseling appointments. At my sessions I began to dig into why I had disregarded my feelings for so long. We identified several points in my life where the "lie" that "feelings don't matter" had been planted.

Being a thinker works very well in the business world. As a leader and particularly one who has lived life in the public eye as a pastor's wife and then as the Founder and CEO of Hearts at Home, this served me well. Where it didn't work so well was at home, in my roles as a wife and a mother. My avoiding-emotion fade started with a *guarded heart* (private, reluctant to share or be open emotionally), which caused a *disconnect in relationship* that resulted in *emotional distance*. How do you turn that around? With vulnerability. That's scary stuff for an avoider like me.

Mark: It was during this time that Jill and I began reading the Yerkoviches' book *How We Love*. As she shared earlier in the book, Jill identified with the Avoider love style, one of five styles they discussed in the book. That book was transformational for us. It was crazy hard for Jill to learn to open up, but it was crazy cool that she did, and I began to see that she really did need me. I, too, realized how much pressure I had put on her to move so far outside herself. I was forcing and demanding her to be someone she wasn't, and that isn't love at all.

Jill: I turned a corner one morning shortly after Mark came home. I had been encouraging a friend who was walking the same journey I had been on. Her husband had left her for another woman. We prayed for, texted, and encouraged each other during that dark season in each of our lives. However, her story wasn't ending like mine was. Her husband never returned home. On the morning that reality became fully evident to her, she texted me. I was in the kitchen when I read the text and my heart was so broken for my friend. I began to cry.

Mark was sitting in the family room, one room away from where I was. I wanted to go upstairs and cry in my bedroom. That's what I'd done the first forty-eight years of my life and the first twenty-nine years of my marriage. But I knew this was my opportunity to do something

I was beyond grateful that Jill was trusting me with her heart.

different. It was time to apply what I was learning.

Reluctantly, I went into the family room, showed Mark the text, and then crawled into his lap and cried my eyes out. It was a new experience for me, but it was a practical step I took to actively change how I operated in our relationship. Over the years, I have learned that sometimes you have to push through awkward to get to a new normal. I did that that day, and I'm so glad I did, because being vulnerable with Mark is now starting to feel normal.

Mark: I was beyond grateful that Jill was trusting me with her heart. I held her and knew that she had taken a risk, and I wanted her to feel safe and secure in making her needs known. This moment was amazing to me. She yielded herself to me and it was beautiful. I was absolutely fulfilled in her actions.

Jill: Mark made it safe for me to step out of my comfort zone. Avoiders are uncomfortable exposing their thoughts and feelings. If you're an avoider who is also an introvert, *and* an internal processor like I am, it's triple hard!

When your spouse struggles with vulnerability, it's extremely important that you are present and reassuring, asking very few questions but just letting them know you can be trusted with whatever is being shared.

Mark: We finally are starting to experience the emotional intimacy I've always longed for us to have. It's taken us more than thirty years, but we're getting there!

NAKED BUT NOT ASHAMED

It was a brief moment of heaven on earth. God had just created Adam and Eve and they were living in the garden of Eden. The Bible tells us they were both naked and were not ashamed (Genesis 2:25 ESV). It was vulnerability's finest moment in human history!

Being naked with one another—both physically and emotionally— is the way God created us to be. It is core to our design and foundational to both our relationship with God and our spouse. It makes sense, then, when I was at Willow Creek's Leadership Summit and heard author, speaker, and researcher Brené Brown say that "vulnerability is the birthplace of everything we hunger for." Closeness. Intimacy. Being heard. Loving. Being loved. Human existence began by being emotionally and physically naked with one another.

Enter the snake, and this is where our struggles with vulnerability began. Satan slithered into the garden, disguised as if he belonged there, and whispered one core lie to Eve that we still struggle with today: *Things that are forbidden by God will fulfill and satisfy you while giving you control and relief from emotional pain.* You can remember it this way: *Where God says no, Satan says go.* This is why we have so many idols in this life: people, food, alcohol, control, pornography, the list goes on. We're still believing that initial lie that God hasn't given us everything we need.

God told Adam and Eve they could eat from any plant in the garden except for one tree. Satan's lies caused Eve to question God's directions. Eventually she and Adam ate the forbidden fruit, believing it would give them more than they already had. After they fell for the lie, they saw they were naked and felt the need to cover up and control the

. . . .

situation. The *lie* of not having enough spawned the *fear* of nakedness that caused the *illusion* of control.

Lies stop us from vulnerability. *He'll never want me if he knows I'm damaged goods. She'll never forgive me if I tell her what I did. He can't love this weak part of me that still struggles. She won't respect me if she knows about this part of my past.* These lies keep vulnerability buried deep under our insecurities. They keep honesty from happening.

Fear stops us from vulnerability. *I'm afraid she'll leave if I get honest. I'm afraid I'll appear weak. I'm terrified she'll lose all respect for me. I'm scared he'll think less of me. I'm afraid this is too big for forgiveness. I'm afraid it will get harder before it gets better. I'm so embarrassed.* Fear keeps us from the intimacy we desire. If we conceal, we stop the real.

Illusions stop us from being vulnerable. *I'll just go to this website for a few minutes . . . no one will know. If I only tell her part of the truth, she'll never find out the rest. I'm strong and independent; I don't need anyone. I'm happy just the way I am; I don't need to change.* Illusions give us the false picture that we have it all under control. They keep us believing that covering up and protecting ourselves is the right way to function.

When we work to stop avoiding emotion, we are also stopping the Perfection Infection in our marriage. Remember, the Perfection Infection happens when we have unrealistic expectations of ourselves and others, and when we unfairly compare ourselves and others. The Perfection Infection keeps us bound up in chains of perfection instead of being free in authenticity.

True intimacy involves both knowing and being known in all our imperfection. It requires **humility** to stop the illusions and see things as they really are, **wisdom** to tackle the lies, **courage** to push through the fear, **compassion** to be safe for your spouse to be honest with, **acceptance** to be able to embrace your and your spouse's messy reality, **forgiveness** to handle the disappointments, **grace** to embrace your shared humanity, and **love** to bear, believe, hope, and endure all things you experience as you move from trying to "be perfect" to "being perfected" and more like Christ each and every day.

THE ART OF BEING HUMAN

When I (Mark) was growing up, I lived within a mile of the Indianapolis 500 Motor Speedway racetrack. I loved the race and would go to the practices, the qualifications, and often the race. One year a race fan jumped onto the racetrack and ran around the track naked until he was escorted away by security. It's possible you're feeling we're suggesting you need to strip down and run naked around the track of your marriage! Well, emotional nakedness does make physical nakedness so much better, and we want both for every married couple, but we've learned it's better off to start building your vulnerability muscle in small ways. Pick two or three of these practical steps to start connecting in a deeper way:

Share your day. Not just what happened but how you *feel* about what happened. Ask your spouse about their day and how he or she feels about it.

Open your eyes during lovemaking. Open your eyes and really look into the eyes of your loved one. It may feel awkward, but don't go backward! Keep moving forward. As you push through awkward, you'll create that new normal!

Resist the urge to move quickly through uncomfortable feelings.

. . . .

Learn to sit with pain. Feel, don't rush to fix. Respond to yourself and your spouse with empathetic statements like, "I'm so sorry," or "That must have been very painful."

Prepare your spouse to listen. Start your sharing with, "I'm learning how to flex my vulnerability muscle, so I'm going to share something with you that scares me." Or, "I'm going to share my feelings about this and I just need you to listen, not to offer ideas for fixing it." This helps your spouse know you're stepping into unfamiliar territory.

Ask for help. Stop playing the martyr and make your needs known. Do this using assertive requests rather than passive-aggressive hints. Even if your spouse doesn't respond with help, you are still learning how to be comfortable in the vulnerability zone of having needs.

When you said, "I do," you linked arms with another human being.

Resist the urge to reveal information in layers. This is a common pattern when "confessing" something your spouse deserves to know. However, it lengthens the healing process and makes building trust even harder. Instead, be completely honest with whatever you need to share. Resist the urge to share 50 percent now and more information later.

See your spouse. Really see him or her. Look beyond the words and notice how he or she really seems to be doing.

Embrace the concept of "shared humanity." Resist the feelings of embarrassment and remind yourself that you're both learning how to navigate the human experience.

Move from thinking you're "independent" to embracing the fact that you're "interdependent." When you said, "I do," you linked arms with another human being.

....

Reframe vulnerability as a strength. Too many of us think of having needs, sharing fears, and having emotions as a weakness, when it's actually a strength.

Stop stonewalling. When we stonewall, we shut down or distance ourselves rather than ask for what we need. This moves us away from instead of toward one another.

Tackle the lies of shame and insecurity. These rob you of being confident in sharing the real you. Rejection is real but often it is also perceived when we look at relationships through the lens of shame and insecurity. If necessary, make an appointment with a Christian counselor to dig into this.

"FOMO"

The first time I (Jill) saw the term FOMO used was when our son Evan sent it in a text one Thanksgiving. He had recently moved to California and was just too poor and too far away to come home for the holidays. We sent him pictures of our celebration and told him we missed him. He wrote back that he had a bad case of FOMO. I asked what that was and he responded: *Fear of Missing Out.*

I've thought about that phrase since then and have come to the conclusion that in order to stop avoiding emotion, I think we need some healthy fear of missing out in our marriage. *If I don't share what I'm really feeling or struggling with, what will I miss out on in our marriage? If I don't get honest with my partner, what intimacy and depth will I keep from happening in our relationship? If I keep this wall up, will my spouse be increasingly tempted to find connection somewhere else? If I continue in self-sufficiency, how will my spouse know that I really do need him/*

her? If I resist getting naked emotionally, what will we miss out on by not tackling the hard stuff of life together?

These are questions we desperately need to ask ourselves. They motivate us to make the changes we need to make. They inspire us to move from a 1.0 fearful-of-being-vulnerable model of ourselves to a 2.0 courageous-honest-and-open model of ourselves that has learned the risk and the result are worth it. These questions spur us on to **courage**, sharing our fears, our needs, and our wounds. When we're afraid of missing out on all that marriage offers, we're inspired to end the masquerade and remove our masks for good. When we can do that, we can truly experience the freedom of being real together!

❖ THINK ABOUT IT ❖

What about you? Do you feel emotionally disconnected from your spouse? Are you the one who avoids emotion? What can you do to become more vulnerable yourself? What can you do to make it safer for your spouse to be vulnerable?

❖ TALK ABOUT IT ❖

My biggest takeaway from this chapter was_____

_____

Looking at the practical steps for building the vulnerability muscle, the two I'd like to try are_____

_____

After reading this chapter, I realize that in order to increase vulnerability, I most need to use my tool of_____

_____

⚜ TALK TO GOD ABOUT IT ⚜

Lord, I had no idea I was keeping so much to myself. I've allowed fear to keep me from sharing my whole self with _____. Help me to recognize the lies I've been believing. Give me courage to push through the fear of being honest. Show me how to be safe for _____ to be honest with me, responding in love and grace rather than anger and criticism. Lord, I've even tried to hide from You. Help me to need You more, trust You more, and become more like You each and every day. In Jesus' Name. Amen.

Today's Truth: "Therefore, confess your sins to one another and pray for one another, that you may be healed."
JAMES 5:16 ESV

## CHAPTER 11

CONTENTMENT, FREEDOM, AND *Hope*

Nearly every morning since our ten-day No More Perfect Marriages blog series, there's a new email in our inbox asking for prayer, encouragement, and hope from a desperate husband or wife facing a crisis in their marriage. Sometimes there are two or three. Most often the story includes infidelity, but sometimes it's just that the slow fades have taken their toll and led one of them to declare, "I don't love you anymore."

Marriage is tough. There's no doubt about it. All couples experience hills and valleys. The good is very good, and the bad can be very, very difficult. Even without crisis, the sameness of day-in-day-out togetherness makes every one of us want to give up at some time or another.

If we'll stick with God, we'll learn to embrace this beautiful work in progress. We'll better understand that we can only change ourselves. We'll embrace the reality that our deepest frustrations are a gold-engraved invitation for us to confront ourselves and look at our own "stuff." We'll discover that getting our way is not nearly as important as finding God's way. And if we stay committed, we'll find that the reality of marriage is far richer and far more rewarding than we ever could have guessed!

RELATIONAL RENOVATION

We finished our kitchen exactly one week before we finished this book. The green gingham wallpaper is now replaced by chocolate brown paint. The old ceramic tile countertop has given way to a speckled cream and brown quartz. Our old cabinets look new now that they have been painted and glazed and have some crown molding added to them. The green door to the garage and our green island add a splash of color to the room. The wall we tore down has now opened up our staircase, which boasts new carpet on the steps and paint on the risers. We've put a lot of hard work into this transformation. When we walk in there, we can hardly believe it's the same kitchen.

It's actually a pretty accurate visual representation of our marriage. We've peeled away layers and layers of junk in the trunk that needed to go. We've repaired broken parts and put a fresh coat of compassion and love on our relationship. We've torn down emotional walls and opened up our hearts to each other. We've gotten rid of what wasn't needed anymore and added new relational furniture where it was needed. We've put a lot of hard work into this transformation. Sometimes we can hardly believe we're the same people.

Of course the tough stuff hasn't gone away. It's still there, but we're dealing with it differently. And the fades? They're there, too. We're just catching them quicker than we used to. We haven't arrived and neither have you. Until the day you get your promotion to heaven, God will use marriage to mature you. You'll

It's the nature of relationship. We naturally pull apart unless we work to stay together.

become more familiar with your God-given tools and pull them out quicker. To some extent, though, you'll always struggle between "what you feel like doing" and "what God wants you to do." This is what it looks like when God is maturing or perfecting you.

REGULAR MAINTENANCE

The fades still creep in to our marriage and they'll creep in to yours too. It's the nature of relationship. We naturally pull apart unless we work to stay together.

In the same way our kitchen will need to be maintained and cared for, our marriage will require time, energy, and effort to keep the fades from reappearing. Unrealistic expectations will creep in when we forget to communicate our hopes and desires with each other. If we disregard what our spouse is communicating or if we neglect to communicate what we are feeling, minimizing will happen. Not accepting will gain ground when one of us tries to change the other. Disagreement will show up when we forget it's more important to do right than to be right. When we're tempted to debate rather than dialogue, we'll have to intentionally stop being defensive because it will inevitably creep in when we're tired, prideful, or fall back into old habits. Naïveté will invariably show up when one or both of us get lax about protecting our marriage. Of course, there will certainly be times we're tempted to keep something from the other—and that's when avoiding emotion will start to happen.

As much as they are similar, there's one major difference between our kitchen makeover and our marriage makeover. The construction tools that spent ten months in our kitchen are now tucked away and unseen, but the God-tools we used for our marriage makeover are still very visible. In fact, we use them every day. We pull out **courage** every time we're tempted to revert back to old, unhealthy ways of relating. **Grace** is used when we bump into each other's imperfections. **Forgiveness** when we disappoint each other. **Humility** reminds us that we are both imperfect and human and that marriage is really about our shared humanity. **Wisdom** keeps us growing and learning and seeking out truth. **Acceptance** helps us to come back to our beginning with the declaration that "I love you just as you are." **Compassion** is used when we need to build a bridge into each other's reality. And **love** is what we pull out when we need to choose to be patient, kind, gentle, and sometimes even long-suffering with each other.

These Christlike responses allow for failure. They embrace authenticity. They break the chains of unrealistic expectations and unfair comparisons. They acknowledge we're both in the perfecting process.

The more we use our God-given tools and work to stop our fades, the more we'll experience *contentment*. We'll discover we're not as alone as we sometimes think. We'll realize the grass really isn't greener on the other side of the fence. We'll embrace our very real spouse and our very real marriage.

········

We'll also find *freedom*. The freedom to be ourselves. The freedom to grow, change, and mature. The freedom to be real with one another. And as we embrace being perfected, the freedom found in Jesus Christ.

Finally we'll experience *hope*. Hope for surviving hard seasons. Hope that God can do His best work through the cracks in our lives. Hope that, with God's help, a broken marriage can be restored and a good marriage can become great.

There are no perfect marriages, but there is a God who wants to "perfect" us through this thing called marriage. When that happens, we get to experience the freedom of being real together!

PERSONAL OPERATING
SYSTEM *Inventory*

This quiz helps you determine your "operating system" traits that are discussed in chapter 6. (Note: This quiz is also available online at www.NoMorePerfectMarriages.com)

For each trait that makes up our personality, there are some evaluating questions in groups of two. Read each question and determine which statement best describes you. If neither one desc ribes you perfectly, choose the one that comes closer to describing you than the other.

Once you have finished all of the evaluating questions, transfer your results to pages 229–31. Then plot where you are on the spectrum. For instance, if there are seven questions and you get four 1s and three 2s, you're going to be somewhere near the center of the spectrum, slightly left of center. If there are seven questions and you get one 1 and six 2s, you'll plot yourself to the far right of the spectrum.

More 1s   **More 2s**

Understanding where you are on the spectrum helps you to understand if that is a strong personality trait or a less pronounced personality trait.

You can take one trait evaluation at a time and hop back over to chapter 6 to read about that trait and how it affects your relationships or you can take the whole evaluation at once and then go back and read about all of your personality traits and how they affect your marriage. If your spouse is willing to take the inventory, you'll want to have him/her do so. This will allow you to discover differences and have discussions that will allow you to handle them well.

Evaluating Questions for Personality Trait #1 *(These have to do with how you process information)*:

1) When I'm trying to figure something out, I think about all the options.
2) When I'm trying to figure something out, I need to process with someone.

1) I think, think, and think some more.
2) I talk, and talk, and talk some more.

1) I sometimes forget to let my spouse know that I'm thinking about or planning something.
2) My spouse always knows what I'm thinking about!

1) In a group setting, I'm not likely to jump in and start the discussion.
2) In a group setting, I'm likely to be the one to share my thoughts first.

1) I tend to organize what I'm going to say before I say it.
2) I start speaking and let the words take their course.

1) If I have a need, I keep it to myself and try to come up with my own solutions.
2) If I have a need, I call and ask someone to help me think through it.

1) Sometimes I forget to tell others the details of an activity.
2) Sometimes others get annoyed at how much information I share with them.

# of 1s _____
# of 2s _____

Evaluating Questions for Personality Trait #2 *(These have to do with how you are emotionally refueled)*:

1) I prefer one-on-one conversations.
2) I prefer group conversations.

. . . .

1) I prefer texting conversations.
2) I prefer talking on the phone or in person.

1) I enjoy solitude.
2) I love a great party.

1) I enjoy work that allows me to dive in with few interruptions.
2) I love activity and working in a group environment.

1) I like to celebrate birthdays on a small scale with just a few family and friends.
2) It's a birthday . . . let's party!

1) I have one hobby.
2) I enjoy several hobbies.

1) I am refueled by being alone.
2) I am refueled by being with people.

# of 1s _____
# of 2s _____

Evaluating Questions for Personality Trait #3 *(These have to do with your physical and emotional capacity):*

1) I prefer to keep my schedule simple and manageable.
2) My calendar is full . . . maybe too full at times.

. . . .

1) I so wish I had more energy.
2) I'm rarely low on energy.

1) I can only focus on and handle a few things at a time.
2) I can juggle many things and multitask easily.

1) I'm careful about how much I say yes to, because I know my limits.
2) It sometimes feels like I'm doing more of the work at home or in a group than others.

1) I love doing nothing on occasion.
2) There's always something that needs to be done.

1) I love to listen to my spouse.
2) I love to help my spouse do something.

1) I struggle with thinking I should be doing so much more.
2) I forget to slow down and just hang out with the family without an agenda.

# of 1s _____
# of 2s _____

Evaluating Questions for Personality Trait #4 *(These have to do with how you organize things):*

1) I'm a filer, not a piler.
2) I'm more often a piler than a filer.

. . . .

1) I have one "to-do" list that keeps me organized.
2) I use sticky notes for everything.

1) I love the peacefulness of order.
2) I enjoy and am comfortable with an imperfect, messy home environment.

1) I know where things are. I don't have to see them to remember them.
2) If I don't see something, I might forget about it. (Out of sight, out of mind.)

1) I love having close to nothing on my desk at work or kitchen counters at home.
2) I have a lot of stuff on my desk or kitchen counters.

1) Everything has a home—you just put things in their home.
2) Sometimes I don't know what to do with all my stuff.

1) I love to store things in bins with clear labels on the outside.
2) I have an "everything drawer" that I sort through to find what I'm looking for.

# of 1s _____
# of 2s _____

Evaluating Questions for Personality Trait #5 *(These have to do with how you manage your time):*

1) I hardly use a calendar.
2) I can't live without my calendar!

1) I often don't have a plan for the day. I wait to see how I'm feeling.
2) I have a plan for tomorrow already in my head.

1) If someone makes a suggestion to do something, I might jump at the opportunity.
2) If someone makes a suggestion to do something, I might have trouble making the change in my mind.

1) Too often I go to the store and forget something I needed because my list is a bit disorganized and might be on the back of a napkin.
2) I occasionally forget something I need at the store, but not very often because I have a very detailed list I use as I shop.

1) I'd love to take advantage of free festivals in the area, but I always seem to miss them.
2) If there's something I want to do, it's on my calendar and I plan for it.

1) Spontaneity and I are like chocolate and peanut butter.
2) Spontaneity and I are like oil and water.

# of 1s _____
# of 2s _____

. . . .

Evaluating Questions for Personality Trait #6 *(This has to do with your preference for thinking or feeling)*:

1) When I need to make a decision, I gather all my facts.
2) When I need to make a decision, I often have a gut feeling about what to do.

1) If I decide to do a project, I finish it no matter how I feel.
2) If I decide to do a project, I work on it when I feel like it.

1) My spouse has told me I'm insensitive.
2) My spouse has told me I'm too sensitive.

1) If someone asks me how I feel about something, I often don't know.
2) If someone asks me how I feel about something, I'm usually able to describe my emotions.

1) Feelings don't matter; only facts matter.
2) Feelings matter . . . a lot!

1) Sometimes I miss subtle nonverbal cues.
2) I'm pretty discerning about reading between the lines on how someone is feeling.

1) I tend to believe we should "buck up" when things get hard.
2) I feel deeply—both my pain and the pain of others.

# of 1s _____
# of 2s _____

. . . .

Personality Trait #1

of 1s _____
# of 2s _____

If you have more 1s, you are likely an Internal Processing Person.
If you have more 2s, you are likely an External Processing Person.

So where are you on the spectrum? Draw a line and plot where you are.

More 1s   **More 2s**

Personality Trait #2

of 1s _____
# of 2s _____

More 1s—you're probably more of an Introvert.
More 2s—you're probably more of an Extrovert.

So where are you on the spectrum? Draw a line and plot where you are.

More 1s   **More 2s**

Personality Trait #3

\# of 1s _____

\# of 2s _____

If you have more 1s, you are likely a Medium-Low Capacity Person.
If you have more 2s, you are likely a Medium-High Capacity Person.

So where are you on the spectrum? Draw a line and plot where you are.

More 1s   **More 2s**

⬅━━━━━━━━━━━━━━━━━━━━━━━━━➡

Personality Trait #4

\# of 1s _____

\# of 2s _____

If you have more 1s, when it comes to organization, you are an Innie.
If you have more 2s, when it comes to organization, you are an Outie.

So where are you on the spectrum? Draw a line and plot where you are.

More 1s   **More 2s**

⬅━━━━━━━━━━━━━━━━━━━━━━━━━➡

Personality Trait #5

\# of 1s _____

\# of 2s _____

If you have more 1s, you're likely Spontaneous.
If you have more 2s, you're likely Structured.

So where are you on the spectrum? Draw a line and plot where you are.

More 1s   **More 2s**

⬅━━━━━━━━━━━━━━━━━━━━━━━━━━━➡

Personality Trait #6

of 1s _____
# of 2s _____

If you have more 1s, you're likely a Thinker.
If you have more 2s, you're likely a Feeler.

So where are you on the spectrum? Draw a line and plot where you are.

More 1s   **More 2s**

⬅━━━━━━━━━━━━━━━━━━━━━━━━━━━➡

"I praise you because I am fearfully and wonderfully made!"
PSALM 139:14

DISCUSSION GUIDE

*D*ear Leader,

This book is designed to be read alone or studied in a small-group setting. It can be a used in a couples group, a moms group, a women-only group, or a men-only group.

Whether you are a group of two or a hundred and two, the free online videos will launch the topic of the week, and the discussion questions for each chapter will guide your conversation following the video. Our hope is that we will give you the tools to lead a successful dialogue as your group reads this book together. If you don't know where to start, we've given you a template with which to work. If you are an experienced leader, the discussion questions can serve to enhance your own ideas.

Regardless of whether you meet in a living room or a church building, the most important aspect of gathering together is intentionally building relationships. You'll notice that each week has a consistent format for discussion. Each section serves a purpose in relationship building:

Video (6–10 minutes)

If you are comfortable doing so, open each gathering with prayer. Commit your time to the Lord and ask Him to lead your conversation. If you aren't comfortable praying aloud, you can ask someone else in the group to pray or you can allow God to use this as an opportunity to stretch and grow you!

When a group first gets together each week, it is beneficial to start out with a video. Each video is available for free online at www.NoMorePerfect.com and is designed to focus everyone in on the topic at hand. The videos are six to ten minutes in length, just enough time to introduce the topic and add some additional perspective to each chapter.

Dig Deep (20–45 minutes)

These questions are designed to facilitate discussion. The best groups are not led by leaders who like to hear themselves talk but rather by leaders who like to hear others talk. There's nothing for you to "teach"; that's what the book is for. Your job is to ask questions that help to drive the discussion and life application deeper. You'll also want to lead by example in answering the questions yourself.

If you are leading the discussion, you'll want to familiarize yourself ahead of time with the questions. As you read the chapter yourself, jot down additional questions you might present to the group. Make sure you pray for your group and for God's guidance as you lead the discussion.

Apply (5–10 minutes)

The "Apply" section is designed for personal reflection and then for goal setting. This helps the reader take all the information they've read and determine what one "nugget" they are going to own. This is the application to daily life that moves us to action. You can review these application suggestions, encouraging each group member to use them to apply what they're learning to their marriage.

Pray

You can choose to have one person close in prayer or have a group prayer time. You can use the prayer included in the discussion guide or pray as you're led.

Remember, in the same way that there are no more perfect marriages, there are also no perfect leaders. Don't put unneeded pressure on yourself to be the perfect leader. It's far more important that you are an honest, authentic leader. Relax, trust God to lead you, share honestly, laugh, and have a good time discussing the book together.

CHAPTER 1

Connect
Have everyone share with the group how they met their spouse.

Dig Deep
Can you (with your spouse's permission) share a time when the rose-colored glasses came off and you thought to yourself, *This isn't what I thought marriage would look like?*

What do you find to be the best part of marriage?

What do you find to be the hardest part of marriage?

Of the slow fades mentioned on pages 20–21, which one—just by looking at the title—resonates with your experience?

Have someone in the group read Ephesians 4:27 and John 10:10. Can you identify any ways you have allowed the devil to get a foothold in your relationship?

Apply
Talk to God this week about your marriage. Remember, He sees. He knows. He cares. He is bigger than any tough place you're experiencing right now.

Text intentionally with your spouse this week. If you're able to, text each other several times during the workday. In marriage, the little things are usually the big things. Texting may seem cumbersome or silly or hard to remember, but it's a great way to stay on each other's mind throughout the day

Take the "How We Love" Quiz (www.howwelove.com) mentioned in the next chapter in order to be ready for next week's discussion!

Pray

Lord, thank You for the gift of marriage. Thank You for this study. Open our hearts up to what You want us to learn and where You want us to grow. Help us to identify the masks we wear and to see that they really are thinly veiled attempts to cover up our imperfections. Show us how to accept "imperfect" in ourselves and in our spouse, and to embrace the process of both of us being perfected by You. In Jesus' Name. Amen.

CHAPTER 2

Connect
Share with the group where you went on your honeymoon and one memory you have from that time. (If you didn't go on a honeymoon, share about why you made that decision and one memory from the early months of your marriage.)

Dig Deep
Describe your growing-up years and the blueprint you brought into marriage.

What did your home internship (blueprint) teach you positively about marriage?

What did your home internship teach you negatively about marriage? Is there anything you need to do a new internship in?

What did you learn about yourself when you took the "How We Love" Quiz? Was this surprising? Did your spouse take the quiz? What did he/she learn?

What was your biggest takeaway from this chapter?

Apply
Just for today, take one step toward your new internship. Pick up a book from the library on the issue. Look up Scripture on the topic (e.g.,

. . . .

Google "Scripture about anger" or "Bible verses about criticism" or "what the Bible says about insecurity"). If needed, set up a counseling appointment to begin to dig through it.

Ask God to show you moments in your blueprint when lies were planted that might be affecting how to see God, how you see yourself, and how you see your spouse.

Take those moments and begin to replace the lies with God's truth from the Bible. (Again, Google can come in handy. Let's say you have identified that somewhere the lie was planted that God can't be trusted. You can search "Bible verses about trusting God," and you'll find God's promises for you!)

Get a date night on the calendar for the two of you.

Pray

Father, we know You will waste nothing in our lives. Every experience—both good and bad—can be used by You. Help us to honestly examine the presumptions, lies, and expectations we carried into marriage that aren't serving us well. Help us to identify where we need to do new home internships in issues that make a difference in our relationships. More than anything, help us to find our hope and our help in You. In Jesus' Name. Amen.

CHAPTER 3

Connect

What is one of your favorite attributes—or strengths—of your spouse? Or what do you most appreciate about him or her?

Dig Deep

Of the eight God-tools introduced in this chapter, which two do you feel you need to use more often? Why?

Brainstorm together one practical step each person can take to start using one of the tools they need to use more often.

A full apology consists of owning what you did wrong, apologizing specifically, and asking for forgiveness. Are you characterized by offering half-apologies or full apologies? If half, which of those three steps is the hardest one for you to do? Why?

What was your biggest takeaway from this chapter?

Apply

When you find yourself frustrated this week, ask these two questions:

a. Does this hurt me or just irritate me?

b. Does this need to be correct or simply accepted?

Who needs some unhumanable love in your life? Your spouse? Your mother-in-law? One of your kids? A neighbor or coworker? Review

Romans 12:9–21. Which instruction in those verses do you need to put into practice today?

Each God-tool has an accompanying Scripture with it. Write out the Scripture of the two God-tools you need to start using more often on index cards. Put those index cards somewhere where you'll see them on a regular basis. (NOTE: If you're leading the group, you might want to bring index cards to distribute so everyone can write out their Scriptures before they head home.)

Pray

Lord, You have given us a toolbox full of tools that we don't use nearly as often as we should. Motivate us to make changes. When we blow it, help us to back up and start our response over again, using the right tool the second time around. Help us to look at ourselves rather than following the temptation to blame our spouse. More than anything, help us to find our identity in You so we can build our lives and our marriages on the firm foundation of truth. In Jesus' Name. Amen.

CHAPTER 4

Connect
What's the most surprising thing you've learned about marriage?

Dig Deep
What expectations did you come into marriage with that you now realize were unrealistic?

As you read, did you identify any unknown expectations that you can share?

Were there any unspoken expectations you were able to recognize?

From the descriptions on pages 82–83, what do you think your mind style is? What about your spouse? How do you think knowing and understanding this might help your marriage?

Of the healthy expectations on pages 94–95, which one do you most need to focus on? Why?

Apply
Have someone read Philippians 4:8. How does this apply to marriage? What you fertilize will grow. Take some time this week to do a "thought audit" where you honestly ask yourself what kinds of thoughts you're fertilizing. Negative thoughts? Fault-finding thoughts? Blaming thoughts? Or what about loving thoughts? Positive thoughts? Kind

thoughts? Based on Philippians 4:8, what do you need to do with your thoughts?

Start paying attention to your thoughts about your spouse and your marriage. Evaluate if any of them are fueled by unknown, unspoken, unrealistic, or unmet expectations. Pull out your God-tool of courage and share honestly with your spouse about what you are discovering.

If your spouse shares anything with you this week, be safe. Don't over-react. Invite continuing conversation with a response like, "Tell me more."

Pray

Lord, we know that all too often our expectations get in the way. Help us to see everyday challenges through different eyes. Show us how to expect the right things. Help us to stay away from idealism and unrealistic expectations that will only result in our own disappointment and disillusionment. We want to learn how to push our thoughts in the right direction, honor You, and stop the fades in our marriages. In Jesus' Name. Amen.

CHAPTER 5

Connect

Does your marriage have traditional roles (e.g., she does the laundry, he does the yard work), or have you bucked some of those traditional roles for something that works better for both of you? If so, how?

Dig Deep

Can you share a time outside of marriage where you've felt minimized? Can you share a time where you did the minimizing?

Of the two kinds of minimizers identified in this chapter — internal and external — which one do you tend to be? Why do you think you default to that kind of minimizing?

Do you tend to be a fixer or a feeler? What were your initial thoughts as you read about the importance of validating?

How's your pace of life? Is it a pace that allows for giving grace and finding the space needed for nurturing your marriage?

Of the six ways to increase margin and decrease minimizing introduced on pages 108 and 109, which one do you need to get started on tomorrow? What is one practical way to take a step in the right direction?

Apply

Evaluate your own personal pace. What is one step you can personally take today to increase your margin for your marriage?

Start paying attention to the minimizing that goes on inside your head. When you recognize it, work to replace minimizing with validating. It won't be easy, but it is possible! Remember, you're creating a new normal for your relationship!

Write out Ephesians 4:32 on an index card and post it somewhere you'll see it on a regular basis. (NOTE: If you're leading the group, you might want to bring index cards to distribute so everyone can write out their Scriptures before they head home.)

Pray

Lord, sometimes we underestimate the way we respond to one another. Show us how to be sensitive to one another. Help us to step into each other's world and resist labeling different as wrong. Show us the God-tools we need to use each and every day. In Jesus' Name. Amen.

CHAPTER 6

Connect

How have your role models influenced your expectations of marriage?

Dig Deep

What were the results of your POS (Personal Operating System) quiz (see summary table on page 135)? If your spouse took the quiz, what did you find out about each other? (NOTE: Discussing what each person/couple learned and how those discoveries will change the way they interact in their marriage will take up the majority of the discussion time this week.)

What was your biggest takeaway while reading this chapter?

Apply

Start paying attention to what you've learned about yourself and/or your spouse. Embrace who you are. Embrace who your spouse is. Thank God each time you see his/her personal operating system in action.

Identify ways your spouse's operating system balances you out. Tell him or her what you appreciate about their operating system and why it balances you out.

Pray

Lord, help us to remember that differences aren't deficiencies. Remind us that You knit us together with unique personalities and temperaments, and oneness happens when we learn to appreciate those in each other. Help us to be more accepting of one another. Convict our hearts when pride creeps in and wants us to believe our way is the right way. Remind us to speak kindly, filled with grace and love as we interact with one another. In Jesus' Name. Amen.

CHAPTER 7

Connect
What favorite activities do you enjoy doing together as a couple?

Dig Deep
Of the questions suggested to get to the heart of disagreement on pages 142–143, which one do you need to ask yourself more often?

Discuss the six disarming phrases on pages 144–146. Which phrases have you tried, if any? What kind of response did you experience? Do you have any additional words or phrases you can share with the group to help decrease disagreement and increase communication?

Of the proactive strategies listed in this chapter, which strategy have you incorporated? Which do you want to start soon?

What was your biggest takeaway from this chapter?

Apply
Which disagreement fade do you more likely default to?

Disagree→ Control → Crush

Disagree → Argue → Control

Become Passive → Withdraw →Deceive

One of your own? _____ → _____ →

_____

Ask God to help you become more aware when you slip into this fade.

. . . .

Choose one of the Scriptures about the weight of our words on page 144 and write it on an index card. Place that card somewhere you can see it every day. (NOTE: If you're leading the group, you might want to bring index cards to distribute so everyone can write out their Scriptures before they head home.)

Pray very specifically for your spouse this week. If you find it helpful, you can write your prayers out in a notebook or journal.

Pray

Lord, disagreement is part of two imperfect people living under the same roof. We know and understand that. However, the way we respond to disagreement can either bring us closer to each other or move us away from each other. Help us to choose responses that disarm conflict and increase understanding and communication. Help us to think about proactive strategies we can put in place to decrease disagreement and be wise about the way we interact with each other. In Jesus' Name. Amen.

CHAPTER 8

Connect

What is one thing that is on your individual bucket list?

Dig Deep

When you think about your home of origin (your first eighteen years), what experience did you have with anger or defensiveness? What about tone of voice? Have you carried any of those experiences into your marriage?

What is one word that would describe how you handle feedback from your spouse? Why did you choose that word?

What was your biggest takeaway from this chapter?

Apply

1) Get a date on the calendar, or determine when you'll have time to talk on a road trip, and ask each other some of the "reflective feedback" questions on pages 173–175. Think of it as an expedition in your marriage!

2) Identify which tool you need to use more often to stop the fade of defensiveness in your marriage.

Pray

Lord, we confess that we sure do kick into defensive mode very easily. We build walls instead of bridges in our marriage. Help us to receive feedback. Show us how to invite our spouse to keep talking. Give us courage to replace passive-aggressive communication with direct, kind, honest communication. More than anything, though, help us to give positive feedback and encouraging words more often. May we build one another up each and every day. In Jesus' Name. Amen.

CHAPTER 9

Connect

What are the little acts of kindness or thoughtfulness or connectedness that mean the most to you in your marriage? (Another way to look at this is "I love it when we/he/she do/does _____.")

Dig Deep

Before you read this chapter, which mindset did you identify with most: "setting boundaries is important to protect your marriage," or "I'm in control and 'rules' about being with the opposite sex are unnecessary"? Did your mindset change in any way after reading the chapter?

What social media boundaries do you and your spouse have in place? What boundaries are you aware of that other couples have in place?

Of the twenty-one hedges mentioned in this chapter, which one do you need to take action on this week?

Apply

What soul mirages do you entertain in your mind? Confess those to God and ask Him to help you focus on truth rather than lies.

Where are you being naïve as it pertains to your responsibility to protect your marriage? What God-tool do you need to use more often to stop the fade of naïveté?

Pray

Lord, we confess that too often we're naïve about protecting our marriage. We also confess that we're affected by peer pressure more than we realize, because we don't want to be thought of as a prude. Help us to look only at You and what You want us to do. Give us the wisdom to steer clear of temptation. When we're faced with it, help us to run in the opposite direction. May we be intentional about stopping the fade of naïveté and getting serious about protecting our marriages. In Jesus' Name. Amen.

CHAPTER 10

Connect

If you could take a one-week vacation to anywhere in the world, where would you go? Why?

Dig Deep

Was this chapter comfortable for you to read, or was it uncomfortable because you don't particularly like to think about sharing feelings?

Of the practical steps to build your vulnerability muscle listed on pages 209–211, which one are you already doing? Which one do you know you need to start doing? Why?

Talk about this statement: *If I resist getting naked emotionally, I will keep our relationship from being all that it can be.* Do you agree? Disagree? What feeling does that statement cause inside of you?

Apply

Ask God for the courage to share more of your history, thoughts, fears, and struggles with your spouse. Take one step toward doing that this week.

Take an inventory of how and where you've been causing a fade in your marriage by avoiding emotion. Just once this week, push through the fear and trust your spouse by sharing one feeling you're experiencing (about work, parenting, extended family, marriage, etc.) with your spouse.

· · · · · · · ·

Pray

Lord, it's scary to be emotionally naked. Yet You didn't design us to be physically naked in marriage without first being emotionally naked. Help us to know how to share our hearts with one another. Show us how to make it safe for our spouse to share their heart with us. May we be motivated to move from a 1.0 fearful-of-being-vulnerable version of ourselves to a 2.0 courageous-honest-and-open version of ourselves. In Jesus' Name. Amen.

CHAPTER 11

Connect

What's challenging about finding time to talk as a couple? What is one thing you've found works for you for finding time to talk as a couple?

Dig Deep

Where do you struggle the most in marriage with "what you feel like doing" versus "what God wants you to do"?

Overall, what God-tool is the one you most need to use more often? What is one practical step you could take to make that happen more often?

What has been your biggest takeaway from this book?

Apply

Go back to chapter 3 and write out the Scripture that goes with the God-tool you need to use more often. Post that Scripture somewhere you can see it on a regular basis.

Ask God to continue to perfect you, making you more like Jesus Christ every day. Continue to learn to interact and respond to your spouse in new, kind, honest, vulnerable, Christlike ways.

Pray

Lord, this book has required us to dig deep. It's not easy to look at ourselves and to identify ways we need to grow. It's important, though. Keep showing us how to respond to each other in a more loving, godly way. Keep helping us to use our God-tools more often. More than anything though, help us to see how we each contribute to the fades in our marriage and how we each can do our part to stop them. In Jesus' Name. Amen.

ACKNOWLEDGMENTS

*T*his book is a project of collaboration in the truest sense. Not only have we shared our story, but many of our friends have allowed us to share theirs as well. Specifically we want to express our appreciation to:

Every couple who has shared their story, frustrations, joys, and discoveries with us. Your honesty has helped formulate the message of this book.

The fabulous people who make up the Hearts at Home leadership team. It is a joy to serve with such a wonderful group of men and women.

Tom and Sue: Thank you for sharing your lake home! It gave us the perfect place to write. We love you and are so appreciative!

Michelle Nietert: Thank you for pre-reading the book and offering feedback from a counselor's perspective. You helped make it a stronger resource for couples!

Our pre-readers and sticky statement team who gave valuable initial feedback: Scott and Bonnie, Skip and Phyllis, Steve and Cassie, John and Robyn, Lori and Hugh, Megan, Becky, Darlene, Jenn, Sarah, Rebecca, Rochelle, Susan, Tina, Marcia, Marci, Ashley, Pam, Julie, Courtney, Rachel, Thanh, Sheryl, and J'Lynn! You guys rock! Thank you for reading, challenging, adding thoughts, asking questions, creating sticky statements, and making suggestions. You have all made this a better book!

Our prayer team: Thank you for standing in the gap for us while we wrote!

The Moody Publishers team: We love partnering with all of you on our Hearts at Home books! John, Betsey, Zack, and Janis—you are the best!

Our family: Thank you for cheering us on and believing in us. Thank you also for hanging in there through the dark season. We've all had a front-row seat at watching God work!

God: Thank You for redeeming the broken places in our lives and our marriage. You are the Redeemer and the Re-Dreamer! This book is evidence of that!

CONNECT WITH MARK & JILL

*D*ear Reader,
We'd love to hear how this book has encouraged you personally! Let's connect online! Want to keep the encouragement going? Subscribe to Jill's blog and get the #MarriageMonday posts we write together every week. Looking for a speaker for your next marriage event? You can request us as speakers at www.jillsavage.org.

Email (Jill): jill@jillsavage.org
Email (Mark): jamsavage7@yahoo.com
Website and Blog: www.JillSavage.org
Facebook: https://www.facebook.com/jillsavage.author
Twitter (Jill): @jillsavage

Twitter (Mark): @mark_savage
Instagram: @jillsavage.author

Make sure you check out the *No More Perfect Marriages* page at www.NoMorePerfect.com and sign up to receive notification of new *No More Perfect Marriages* resources as they become available! We want to help you share what you've learned and keep the encouragement going!

Joining you in the journey,

Mark and Jill

ABOUT THE AUTHORS

Mark and Jill Savage are passionate about encouraging, educating, and equipping families. After serving in church ministry for twenty years, the Savages are meeting the needs of families as authors and speakers. Known for their honesty, humor, and practical teaching, Mark and Jill bring hope and encouragement to every audience.

Jill is the author of nine books, including *Real Moms . . . Real Jesus* and *No More Perfect Moms*. She coauthored the book *Better Together* with her daughter Anne. Together, Mark and Jill have authored two Hearts at Home books, *Living with Less So Your Family Has More* and *No More Perfect Marriages*. The parents of five adult children and grandparents of three, the Savages make their home in Normal, Illinois.

. . . .

Want to request the Savages to speak at your marriage event?

Want to bring a No More Perfect Marriages event to your church or community?

You can do both at www.JillSavage.org!

HEARTS *at* **HOME**

The Go-To Place for Moms

Hearts at Home is dedicated to giving moms ongoing education and encouragement in every stage of motherhood. One of our most impactful resources is the Hearts at Home Conference experience. The conferences, attended by more than ten thousand women each year, provide a unique, affordable way to refresh your mom batteries. Hearts at Home Conference events make a great weekend getaway for individuals, mom groups, or just to enjoy time with that special friend, sister, or sister-in-law.

In addition to this book and conference events, you can sign up for a free monthly eNewsletter called *Hearts On-The-Go*, visit the Hearts at Home website, blog, and join the conversation on Facebook, Instagram, and Twitter.

Hearts at Home
1509 N. Clinton Blvd.
Bloomington, IL 61701
Phone: (309) 828-MOMS
Email: hearts@HeartsatHome.org
Web: www.HeartsatHome.org
Facebook: heartsathome
Twitter: hearts_at_home
Instagram: heartsathome

. . . .

NOTES

1. Copyright©2007MyRefuseMusic(BMI)(admin.Atwww.capitolcmgpublishing .com) / Club Zoo Music (BMI) / SWECS Music (BMI). All rights reserved. Used by permission.

2. Jill Savage, *No More Perfect Moms: Learn to Love Your Real Life* (Chicago: Moody, 2013), chapter 1.

3. Milan Yerkovich and Kay Yerkovich, *How We Love: Discover Your Love Style, Enhance Your Marriage* (Colorado Springs: WaterBrook, 2008). Used with permission.

4. https://www.howwelove.com/love-styles/.

5. http://gregorc.com/.

6. K. B. Haught, *The God Empowered Wife: How Strong Women Can Help Their Husbands Become Godly Leaders* (Intendion, 2008), 66.

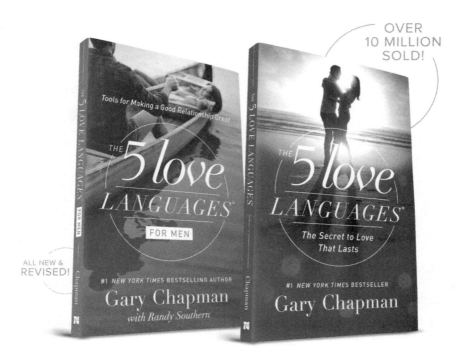

YOU'VE READ THIS ONE—
NOW COMPLETE THE SERIES!

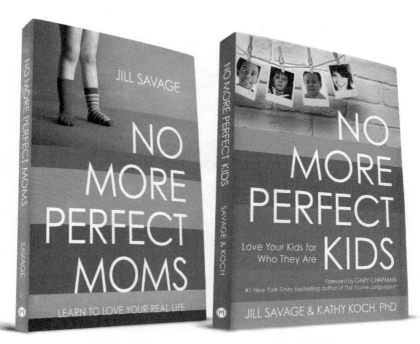

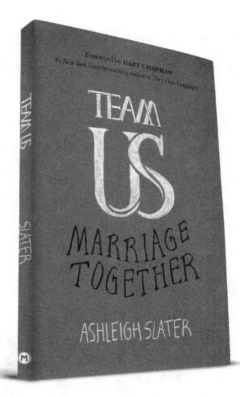

"*Team Us* addresses one of the most important aspects of an intimate marriage—becoming one. With a whimsical and engaging style, Ashleigh Slater challenges us to build our 'team' with careful thought, perseverance, and commitment."

—Gary Thomas, author of *Sacred Marriage* and *A Lifelong Love*

Also available as an eBook.

BEING A MOM IS HARD,
but it doesn't have to be lonely.

Also available as an eBook.